There Is Nothing
Like a Thane!

Gielgud will never be happy vocally with Macbeth; his voice is neither deep enough nor resonant enough. But what sheer acting ability can do, he does.
James Agate.

There Is Nothing Like a Thane!

The Lighter Side of *Macbeth*

Compiled and illustrated by
Clive Francis

 Thomas Dunne Books
St. Martin's Griffin ⚇ New York

Also by Clive Francis

Laughlines
Sir John, The Many Faces of Gielgud
There Is Nothing Like a Dane

For my mother who first opened my eyes to Shakespeare.

THOMAS DUNNE BOOKS.
An imprint of St. Martin's Press.

www.stmartins.com

ISBN 0-312-31379-9

First published in Great Britain by Robson Books

First U.S. Edition: December 2003

10 9 8 7 6 5 4 3 2 1

By the pricking of my thumbs
Something wicked this
way comes.

<small>ACT 4, SCENE 1.</small>

Many of Shakespeare's plays are the
worse for being acted:
Macbeth, for instance.

SAMUEL JOHNSON

Introduction

Fair is foul, and foul is fair ...
Act 1, Scene 1.

One cold afternoon in 1937, Laurence Olivier roared onto the Old Vic stage to face a sparse elderly audience, splattered around the theatre. Sitting bolt upright in one of the side boxes was an eager schoolboy, aglow in anticipation of the story that was about to unfold. Olivier immediately directed his performance towards this diminutive figure, encouraging the rest of the cast to do likewise.

Never had *Macbeth* been so bellowed and shrieked and so enthusiastically over-played, as it was that afternoon.

'This I trust will be a performance he'll never forget,' smiled Olivier in the interval. 'Let's make the second half just as thrilling.'

When the curtain rose, the boy had gone.

Having delved into the lighter side of *Hamlet*, with *There is Nothing Like a Dane!* it was suggested I should have a crack at *Macbeth*, a play which also seems to have an abundant wealth of stories, many of them verging on the outlandish. Charles Kean in 1858, for example, was the first actor to play the Thane in original 10th-century costume, while his wife, on the other hand, insisted on dressing Lady M. in the Victorian fashion of the day – a small discrepancy of 800 years!

Then there was the great William Macready, who, to get himself worked up for the Dunsinane scene, would repeatedly beat his head against a brick wall. Which is just as dramatic as Anthony Sher asking the R.S.C. to track down two professional murderers to advise him on hacking someone to death.

Apart from a rather tired school production, my first memory of the play was seeing my mother perform Lady Macduff at the Winter Gardens Theatre, Eastbourne. It was presented by a wonderful group of Shakespeare enthusiasts with whom, at the age of nine, I had made my first stage appearance as Mustardseed.

The foyer was teeming when I arrived and only by dint of luck was I able to get a seat between two rather corpulent gentlemen. What struck me as strange was why the Eastbourne Shakespeare Society were playing *Macbeth* in the round, or rather within a roped-off arena, and why the majority of the audience were middle-aged men all shouting at each other. Suddenly two huge thugs, wearing nothing but sawn-off leotards, jumped into the ring and began hurling each other about; it was quite apparent I was sitting in the wrong auditorium.

Climbing the stairs to the Starlight Rooms, I entered a very different atmosphere. Meagre collections of people, having dribbled in from the cold, were sitting around in tiny groups, nodding thoughtfully in a contemplative mood. This was truly desperate; the only bursts of excitement being when downstairs landed a score, then a roar of jubilation would rise up through the floor to infiltrate the gloom and doom of Glamis. The next day my mother contracted chicken pox. By the end of the week so had the rest of the cast, and the last night was cancelled!

Macbeth is certainly not a play for the squeamish. It is the blackest, gloomiest and most satanic of all the tragedies. From the moment the hags screech, 'Fair is foul, and foul is fair,' the plot plummets into the depraved and evil world of black magic and witchcraft; and if that isn't enough, the play has more stabbings, murders, deaths and fights than any other – and plenty of blood, in fact buckets of the stuff. Unfortunately none of this worked too well in Shakespeare's favour when *Macbeth* was first performed at Hampton Court, on 7th August 1606. Although James I had a morbid interest in the powers of darkness, he also had a queasy antipathy towards blood and butchery and did not care to be trapped on his throne for over two hours witnessing so many gory scenes.

The evening started badly anyway when Hal Berridge, the boy playing Lady Macbeth, was taken ill and suddenly died backstage – according to James Aubrey, Shakespeare had no choice but to take over the part himself. Thus the curse of *Macbeth* was born, and with it a whole portfolio of theatrical superstitions, many of which are still rigidly obeyed to this very day.

Whistling, for example, is very bad luck in the theatre. This is a superstition that dates back to the 18th and 19th century, when stage staff responsible for the raising and lowering of the scenery were ex-seamen, and the stage manager traditionally directed them by a series of whistles, one for raise and two for lower. Consequently, if anyone else whistled it could cause dangerous confusion.

Anything to do with death is also taboo. No real coffins on stage, for obvious reasons, no real mirrors either, as they're supposed to reflect the Devil standing behind you! Certain colours too are bad luck – yellow, for example, as this is worn by the Devil in mediaeval Mystery Plays and, because of its associations with death, black too. Until not so long ago, actors had their dinner jackets made of midnight blue instead. But the unluckiest of all is green. When actors performed death scenes in the 18th century, a green cloth was placed upon the stage to protect their beautiful clothes, (hence the expression 'see you on the green'.) If the actor were costumed in green as well, he would simply blend into the floor and not be seen.

'If I get a cold in da nose and I hear a raven croaking at da same time, then dat means trouble,' said the legendary Jimmy Durante. Actors have always been superstitious and constantly perform private little rituals to keep themselves safe. For instance, I can never go on stage at an opening performance without kissing the scenery; but then, Thora Hird used to wear three of her daughter's nappy pins under her costume, to bring her luck.

Tallulah Bankhead went even further and insisted that visitors to her dressing room entered with their right foot first, the left being apparently unlucky. Noël Coward's only superstition was 'it is very bad luck to sleep 13 in a bed!' and Robert Morley's 'never drive to the theatre whilst listening to *The Archers.*'

I once heard of a performer who, before an opening night, would lock himself in the loo and recite the names of all his favourite actors. Which is nearly as silly as Leslie Phillips jumping up and down in his dressing room, and burping!

Mind you, it can sometimes work against you. Just before the opening night of his *Hamlet*, in 1951, Alec Guinness popped into the Garrick Club and touched every bust and painting he could find of Shakespeare. The next day the press claimed the production an unmitigated disaster and slated his performance. When Marie Lohr was about to open in Coward's *Waiting in the Wings*, she went to St Mark's Church to pray for a good and successful first night. As she left to return to the theatre, she slipped and broke her arm. 'No good deed ever goes unpunished,' remarked The Master.

But the play considered the unluckiest, and one that still remains fraught with disaster, is *Macbeth*. Actors hardly ever mention it by name, referring to it as 'That Play', 'The Unmentionable', 'The Scottish play'. Or, in Peter O'Toole's case: 'The Harry Lauder Show'. If an actor quotes from it in a dressing room, he must immediately leave the room, turn around three times, break wind and spit – and then ask for permission to re-enter.

One summer's evening in 1865, Abraham Lincoln, President of all America, decided to read *Macbeth* to a small party of close friends. The next day, while sitting in his box at the theatre, he was assassinated. When Laurence Olivier first played the part, in 1937, Lilian Baylis, doyenne of the Old Vic for thirty years, died on the opening night. The following day a seat which Olivier had been sitting on, only seconds earlier, was struck by a falling stage weight and smashed to kindling. The list is endless!

Before a Manchester opening of the play, two actors died of heart attacks, the Third Witch collapsed whilst dancing around her cauldron, and a month later, as a consequence of laryngitis, flu, sackings and a broken toe, four actors had to play the part of Macbeth, in a single week.

When Paul Rogers played the Thane in Moscow in the 1950s, he clashed so violently one afternoon with Macduff that half his claymore flew across the stage and embedded itself in an empty seat; the very seat that President Khrushchev was to occupy three hours later. In 1954, the company manager of a Dublin production broke both his legs, an electrician electrocuted himself, and Banquo tried to commit suicide.

While scenery was being transported into a theatre in Cape Town, an innocent onlooker asked a stage-hand what they were preparing for. 'Macbeth', came the reply, and immediately a bundle of spears dislodged themselves from a ramp, piercing the stranger to death.

Dame Sybil Thorndike played Lady Macbeth at the Prince's Theatre (now the Shaftesbury) in 1926. After a series of terrifying misfortunes within the company and on stage, Dame Sybil had difficulty in controlling her nerves. One evening her husband, Sir Lewis Casson, took her into their dressing room:

> 'Sybil, the devil works in this play. There is
> horror here, we must do something positive
> against it.'

And, together they knelt and read aloud the Ninety-first Psalm, which calmed and strengthened them.

At one time the chief reason for the play's continual list of wretchedness and failures (or 'frosts' as they were known) were bound up chiefly with the music of Matthew Locke. The Singing Witches had been a tradition since Sir William Davenant (Poet Laureate to Charles I) introduced the score in his version of the play, in 1664. All manner of actors and stage hands were ejected from dressing rooms to the streets for daring to hum, or worse, whistle any part of this melodious music, especially its hit number, which began:

> Here's juice of toad and oil of adder;
> These will make the charm grow madder...

The witches were traditionally played by men and performed in what Horace Walpole termed 'a buffoon light.' When Garrick came to revive the play in 1744, he restored a lot of the text, which had been fairly mutilated by Davenant, but, for some reason, kept in the songs and dances for the flying witches – though in his version they did not fly about the stage. Garrick's witches usually wore blue-checked aprons, torn mob-caps and high-crowned black hats.

Another of Davenant's mutilations was the famous Porter scene in Act 2, which Garrick was nervous of reinstating, as he felt that the character's discourse on drink would appeal to the footman's gallery, but no where else in the house.

One of the greatest Lady Macbeths of her day was Sarah Siddons, who first tackled the role in 1785. Just before the performance Sheridan burst into her dressing room demanding to know if it was true that she was about to introduce some new business in the sleep-walking scene. From what he had heard she was about to break tradition with Mrs Pritchard by putting down her candlestick (*unheard* of before) so as to be able to wash the sightless blood from off her hands. Sheridan was adamant that the public would never accept such a strong departure from tradition, but Siddons argued that the hand washing was absolutely necessary and would remain. Right through the play she scored and when the disputed scene arrived she had her greatest triumph of all. The audience were mesmerised and Sheridan the first to congratulate her. Two hundred and sixteen years later, and Sarah Siddons' hand washing still remains one of the great traditional pieces of Shakespearean business, and no other actress has as yet arisen to break it.

When asked for an appraisal of her performance, James Sheridan Knowles remarked, with a sort of shudder, 'Well, sir, let me put it this way, I swear, I smelt the blood.' In 1821, Benjamin Haydon described in his diary an occasion when she recited the entire play to a roomful of admirers:

'Mrs Siddons acts *Macbeth* better than either Kemble or Kean. It is extraordinary the awe this wonderful woman inspires. While we were all eating toast and tinkling cups and saucers, she began again. All noise ceased. It was like the effect of a Mass bell at Madrid. Two or three of the most distinguished men of the day, their eyes full of water from the constraint to hear Mrs Siddons' 'eye of newt and toe of frog' – it was extraordinary and I went away highly gratified. As I stood on the landing to get cool, I overheard my own servant in the hall say: 'Why is that old lady making such a dreadful noise?'

'I'm the worst Macbeth I've ever seen,' wailed Ralph Richardson, possibly the saddest Macbeth of the last century – 'If I were the public, I'd ask for my money back.' The press had hammered his performance quite viciously and rather sadistically. 'A robot player who stumps across the broad stage as if in need of a compass to find the text,' wrote the acerbic Kenneth Tynan. 'Sir Ralph, who seems to me to have become the glass eye in the forehead of English acting, has now bumped into something quite immoveable.'

One afternoon at Stratford, a startled stage manager discovered Richardson waiting in the wings in a long white beard and clutching a staff. 'Sir Ralph,' she whispered frantically, 'we're playing *Macbeth* this afternoon, not *The Tempest*.' 'Are we?' he replied. 'Oh, dear!' – so reluctant was he to play the Thane that he'd come down in the wrong costume and make-up.

Anyway, as to the play itself, which is what this tiny book is all about, how best to describe it? How best to succinctly convey to you its complex and intriguing story … well, I could do no better than quote the *Eastbourne Chronicle* of the 1940s, which summoned up *Macbeth* as:

> 'A story of an ambitious and selfish married
> couple who traffick with the other world for
> their own ends. Set amid the rugged
> grandeur of the Scottish Highlands.'

Clive Francis

An eternal curse fall on you!

ACT 4, SCENE 1.

And of Macbeth, speak nothing,
Nor his name,
nor his play, nor
Its last line, no last line of any play,
For it signifies completion, nothing.

Jonathan Field 1990

My name's Macbeth.

Act 5, Scene 6

This enormous dunghill
Voltaire

Shakespeare demands a rapid pace. He is always in a hurry to tell his tale. The beginning of *Macbeth* is an example of the speed at which Shakespeare works. Macbeth enters, makes one short observation on the weather and is immediately plunged into the drama of murder. Only one second is allowed for the establishment of the character, before events sweep upon him.

Ralph Richardson. *Lecture on 'The Actor',* 1952

Macbeth is not a character of the first rate; all the pitch of it is exhausting in the first and second acts of the play. This judgement is formed from the drowsy and ineffectual manner of David Garrick's predecessors, who could not force attention or applause from the audience during the last three acts.

Dramatic Miscellanies

Shakespeare said of the actor that he was an abstract and brief chronicle of the time. 'Out, out, brief candle!' cries Macbeth.

> 'Life's but a walking shadow; a poor player,
> That struts and frets his hour upon the stage,
> And then is heard no more.'

I do not like being called a candle, even for Shakespeare, and to remind me that I am particularly abstract and brief depresses me!

Ralph Richardson. *Foyle's Luncheon.* 1951

When shall we three meet again?

ACT 1, SCENE 1.

Scene 1 – A blasted heath. A cauldron boiling. Thunder and lightning. Three witches discovered.

FIRST WITCH: When shall we three meet again?
In thunder, lightning, or in rain?

SECOND WITCH: When the hurlyburly's done,
When the battle's lost and won

THIRD WITCH: That will be ere the set of sun.

FIRST WITCH: Where the place?

SECOND WITCH: Upon the heath.

THIRD WITCH: There to meet with Mac-beeth.

FIRST AND SECOND: Mac-beeth?
(A drum sounds off)

THIRD WITCH: (Gasp) A drum, a drum!
                       Macbeth doth come.
(The drum approaches and then fades)

ALL: (Sigh) Oh, well.
(Musical intro starts to the tune of 'There is Nothin' Like a Dame'.)

FIRST WITCH: (Sung) We got moonlight on the heath,
                       We got contagion, mist and fogs.
                       We got bats and rats and lizards
                       And the cutest little frogs.

SECOND WITCH: We got hubble,

THIRD WITCH: We got bubble,

FIRST WITCH: A selection of wolf's banes.

ALL: What ain't we got?
                       We ain't got thanes!

FIRST WITCH: We got wee Moira Anderson,

SECOND WITCH: A football team to make you cringe.

THIRD WITCH: We got lots of lousy stand-up
                       At the Edinburgh Fringe.

FIRST WITCH: We got Lulu,

SECOND WITCH:	Haggis,
THIRD WITCH:	*Trainspotting,*
FIRST WITCH:	Porridge,
SECOND WITCH:	Bagpipes-
ALL:	HELL! What ain't we got? You know darn well!
FIRST WITCH:	*(Recite)* We got nothin' to put on a tall black hat for.
SECOND WITCH:	We got nothin' to groom our old black cat for.
ALL:	There is nothin' like a thane, Nothin' in the world, Not Duncan, Malc or Donalbain Could be anything like a thane.
ALL:	There are no spells like a thane, And nothin' smells like a thane, There are no gays like a thane, And nothin' slays like a thane, There's nothin' built like a thane Or wears a kilt like a thane ...
FIRST WITCH:	*(Spoken)* Royal Stuart Tartan.
SECOND WITCH:	Just above the knee.
ALL:	Lovely!
FIRST WITCH:	*(Sung)* There ain't a thing that's wrong with any weird sister here, That can't be cured by puttin' her near A manly, masculine, big, butch, hunky thane!

THIRD WITCH:	*(Swoons)* Ooooooo!
ALL:	There is nothin' like a thane,
	Nothin' in the world,
	Not jealous Moor or loopy Dane
	Could be

ANY-Y-THING LIKE A THANE!
Malcolm McKee
with apologies to South Pacific and Oscar Hammerstein.

*Swords I smile at, weapons
laugh to scorn ...*
ACT 5, SCENE 6

When Ralph Richardson played Macbeth at Stratford, in 1952, he had great difficulty in remembering the choreographed moves for his duel, and devised his own routine for remembering them. It went something like this:

'One, two, clash swords, three, four and round we go. I lunge at you cocky, now you lunge at me.'

When it came to the actual performance he forgot to keep these instructions to himself, and they were heard in full volume all around the house.

When Noël Coward saw Olivier's performance of Macbeth, he nearly died from laughing.

To know my deed 'twere best not know myself.

ACT 2, SCENE 2.

MACDUFF: Hold it! Are you, perchance, one Macbeth, self-styled monarch of the glen, formerly Thane of Glamis and Cawdor, what three witches put the evil eye on? Whose baby-battering spouse helped you chop King Duncan and blame his honest, law-abiding grooms, before she went potty herself? The one what put the frighteners on the Royal princes, had your mate Banquo professionally rubbished, my wife and chickens rubbed right out, can't sleep, sees woods moving, has a complex about paternal pregnancies, and waffles on and on and on about tomorrow?

MACBETH: Yes.

MACDUFF: Right, lad, you're for the high jump.

Bill Greenwell. *How to be Ridiculously Well-read in One Evening*

I am in blood stepped in so far that, should I wade no more ...

ACT 3, SCENE 4.

According to Timothy West, Peter O'Toole played Macbeth in baseball boots. He received the best laugh of the evening when he came on stage after the murder of Duncan drenched from head to toe in gore. Blood dripped in great dollops from his hands and hair, and also from the points of both daggers. He stood for what seemed an eternity in this gory state, before announcing gravely, 'I have done the deed.'

Macbeth is all about Scotland. Stands to reason, doesn't it? If it'd been about England, Shakespeare would have just have called it Beth.

John Christopher-Wood. *Elsie and Norm's 'Macbeth'.*

Fathered he is, and yet he's fatherless.

ACT 4, SCENE 2.

The actor playing Macbeth died in the midst of an opening night; I don't mean he gave a bad performance; I mean he plain dropped dead.

William Redfield. *Letters from an Actor.*

Black Macbeth will seem as pure as snow ...

ACT 4, SCENE 3.

In 1935 John Houseman hired the twenty-year-old Orson Welles to direct an all-black production of 'Macbeth'. They decided to set it in nineteenth-century Haiti, paying special importance to the supernatural aspects of the play.

Welles and I had chosen the cast together including a graduate of RADA to play Hecate, a composite figure of evil which Welles had assembled out of fragments of witches' lines and to whose sinister equipment he presently added a twelve-foot bullwhip. Our supernatural department was very strong. In addition to the witches we had a troupe of African drummers commanded by Asdata, the late minister of culture of the Republic of Sierra Leone. Except for their leader, who had a flawless Oxford accent, they spoke little English: the star of the troupe, Abdul, an authentic witch doctor, seemed to know no language at all except magic. Their first act, after they had been cast in *Macbeth*, was to file a formal requisition for five live black goats. These were brought into the theatre by night and sacrificed, hugger-mugger, according to approved tribal ritual, before being stretched into resonant drum skins.

One day, after Orson, Virgil (Thomson) and I had been auditioning their voodoo numbers, we complained to Asdata that his chants did not sound evil enough. Virgil, as usual, got right down to the point.

'Are those real voodoo?'

'Oh, yes. Yes, indeed, Sirs. That is real, authentic voodoo.'

'They don't sound wicked enough.'

'Sirs, I ...'

'Sometimes for the theatre you have to exaggerate.'

'I am sorry, Sirs. You can't be any more wicked than that!'

Finally Asadata admitted what those chants of his were: they were strong spells intended to ward off beriberi – not to induce it. He dared not give us the real thing, he explained. It might have worked.

[Even after its successful opening the spells continued to ward off evil. But when Percy Hammond, drama critic of the Herald Tribune, *attacked the Negro Theatre as an 'exhibition of deluxe boondoggling,' he failed to reckon with the consequences.]*

Early in the afternoon of April 15th, the day of the *Macbeth* reviews, Orson and I were formally visited in my office by Asadata and his corps of African drummers, including Abdul, the authentic witch doctor. He produced a sheaf of clippings from which he detached the *Herald Tribune* review.

'The work of an enemy?'

'The work of an enemy.'

'He is a bad man?'

'A bad man.'

Asadata nodded. His face was grim as he turned to his troupe, to Abdul in particular and repeated what I had said. The men nodded, then silently withdrew. Excited by waves of praise and a line a block long at the box office, we quickly forgot about them and Percy Hammond.

When we arrived at the theatre the next day our disturbed house manager reported to us that the basement had been filled, during the night, with unusual drumming and with chants more weird and horrible than anything that had been heard on stage. Orson and I looked at each other for an instant, then quickly away again, for in the afternoon paper which we had picked up on our way uptown was a brief item announcing the sudden illness of the well-known theatre critic, Percy Hammond. He died some days later – of pneumonia, it was said.

John Houseman. *Run-Through.*

In 1948 Orson Welles directed and starred in his own film adaptation of *Macbeth*.
He was supposed to have made it in 23 days, I was quite surprised, thought he'd done it
in two.
Joe Orton. *The Diaries*

'Tis safer to be that which we destroy ...

ACT 3, SCENE 2.

When Herbert Beerbohm Tree produced *Macbeth* his stage management recruited 50 real guardsmen as walk-ons and rehearsed them for the battle scene. They entered into the spirit of the occasion and began knocking each other out. So enthusiastic were they for their new-found occupation, that they began chopping great chunks out of the stage. One soldier swung his sword with such force that it cut a huge hole in the scenery. 'Stop!' cried Tree. 'Never hit a backcloth when it's down.'

The multiplying villainies of nature, do swarm upon him.

ACT 1, SCENE 2.

In 1917 Tree built His Majesty's Theatre, where he presented elaborate productions of Shakespeare's plays, in which great attention was paid to the commotions of Nature. Just before his entrance in *Macbeth* there was a long roll of thunder, a roar of wind and a rattle of hail; the darkness was suddenly pierced by blinding flashes of lightning, in which one could see rocks falling and a stout oak-tree, rent to the roots, toppling to the earth; following this the elements howled invisibly for a space; then came an ear-splitting peal of thunder, a final shriek of the blast, and against the dazzling background of the lightning-riven sky stood the figure of Macbeth. Then Shakespeare got a look-in.

Tree was so much concerned with his own performance that nothing else seemed to matter. He stopped in the middle of, 'Tomorrow, and tomorrow ...' to complain to an elderly actor: 'would you kindly oblige me by moving out of the way. Otherwise they won't be able to see me from the Royal box. Thank you.'

Hesketh Pearson. *The Last Actor Managers*

Have we eaten on the insane root ...?

ACT 1, SCENE 3.

Lady Macbeth should be played in a low, anxious voice, and she should move slowly about the stage, with fixed, glaring, open eyes, and with horror struck features.

Francis Gentleman. *1744*

Like a rat without a tail ...

ACT 1, SCENE 3.

In 1920 the young Donald Wolfit was playing minor parts in a touring production of Macbeth. *It was one of his duties on the discovery of the murder of Duncan, to rush on with a lighted torch as one of the servants. All went well 'til they reached the second house on Saturday night. Wolfit takes up the story:*

Fire regulations were not so rigid in those days and as a consequence tow soaked in methylated spirits were allowed in the hand-held torches. Stimulated by the large and enthusiastic audience I was inspired to make this an entrance of great terror and display. I was the last to enter through the archway, which was lit by a large standard lamp. Unfortunately the electrician, thinking everyone had passed, had tightened the cable of the lamp in preparation to unplugging it. With my flaming torch held high, I launched myself through at great speed, passed the electrician like a rocket caught my foot in the cable and hurtled through the air still clasping my torch. I landed at the Thane's feet with my hair ablaze and greeted with a roar of laughter. Macbeth seized my wig, stamped out the flames and ignominiously hauled me off, still completely entangled in yards and yards of cable.

Donald Wolfit.

Doubly redoubled strokes upon the foe ...

ACT 1, SCENE 2.

Olivier used to throw himself into the final combat with such gusto that each of his Macduffs lived in peril of his life. So legend has it, a stagehand used to be positioned in the Old Vic wings to whisper to the hyped-up Olivier: 'Now don't forget, Larry, you're supposed to lose this fight.'

One night the impact was so ferocious that Olivier's sword snapped. Both he and a terrified Macduff watched as its lethal blade flew out into the darkened auditorium. Nervously they waited for the impact from a stricken member of the audience, but all was ominously silent.

Afterwards a little old lady shuffled up to the stage door clutching the offending weapon, and asked if Olivier would kindly autograph it for her.

Better health attend
his majesty!

ACT 3, SCENE 4.

It is said that when the actor Barry Sullivan arrived in Sheffield with a very bad cold and the local stage manager asked him when he would like to rehearse with the resident company, he said he had no intention of rehearsing in his present condition. When reminded that the week's repertoire was a very stiff one – *Hamlet* on Monday, *Richard III* on Tuesday, *Macbeth* on Wednesday, etc – and that the company would at least like a word or two of instruction, he replied, – 'Instruction my foot! Tell them all to keep six feet away from me, and be damned!'

The love that follows us sometime is our trouble,
which still we thank as love.

ACT 1, SCENE 6.

A gentleman was announced for the character of Macbeth, and went through it with so much reputation that it was agreed to give it out the following night. A Miss Budgel played Lady Macbeth, and it so happened that during his acquaintance with this lady, at the different rehearsals, he fell passionately in love with her. During the time of the performance he was more enraptured than ever. After it was over no one could be found to announce a repetition of the play for the following night. 'God bless me,' cried Macbeth, 'what shall we do?' 'My dear sir, said Miss Budgel, 'you have nothing for it but to give it out yourself.' 'My dear creature,' returned the charmed Macbeth, 'I'll do it – my sweet Miss Budgel – dear, charming Miss Budgel!' On he rushed, full of Miss Budgel, and, as soon as he could be heard, thundered out. 'Ladies and gentlemen, tomorrow evening – Miss Budgel will be done over again.'

Charles Dibdin. *A Musical Tour.* 1788.

Screw your courage to the sticking place
ACT 1, SCENE 7.

The American actor Edwin Forrest experienced great success when he appeared at Drury lane in the 1830s, overshadowing Macready's enormous popularity. Sparked by jealousies, the two actors entered into an open feud. This climaxed in 1849 when Forrest instigated a riot outside the Astor Place Opera House, New York. Macready described the occasion in his diary.

I went on; they would not let me speak. Someone flung a rotten egg close to me. I pointed it out to the audience and smiled with contempt, persisting in my endeavour to be heard. At last there was nothing for it, and I said: 'Go on,' and the play proceeded in dumb show. Copper cents were thrown, some struck me, four or five eggs, a great many apples, nearly – if not quite – a peck of potatoes, lemons, pieces of wood, a bottle of asafetida (a vile pungent gum), which splashed my own dress, smelling of course most horribly. The second act closed in exactly the same way. I dressed for the third and went on; the tumult was the same, the missiles growing thicker. At last a chair was thrown from the gallery on to the stage, and another into the orchestra pit, which made the remaining musicians move out. The police rushed in, closed upon the scoundrels occupying the centre seats and seemed to lift or bundle them in a body out of the house, amid the cheers of the audience. The bombardment outside now began. Stones were hurled against the windows in Eighth Street, smashing many; volleys of stones flew without intermission, battering and smashing all before them. The banquet scene was partially heard and applauded. I went down to change my dress, the battering at the building, doors and windows growing louder and louder. Water was running down fast from the ceiling to the floor and making a pool there. The audience removed themselves for protection behind the walls; the house, as you can imagine, was considerably thinned. I flung my whole soul into every word I uttered, acting my very best and exciting the audience to a sympathy even with the glowing words of fiction, whilst these dreadful deeds of real crime and outrage were roaring at intervals into our ears and rising to madness all round us. The death of Macbeth was loudly cheered.

Suddenly we heard a volley of musketry. 'What's that?' I asked. 'The soldiers have fired.' Another volley came, and another. News came that several were killed. It was believed that at least twenty-two had perished, and so I quitted the New York stage.

At last a chair was thrown from the gallery on to the stage, and another into the orchestra pit, which made the remaining musicians move out.

I am faint; my gashes cry for help.
ACT 1, SCENE 2.

FEBRUARY 28th
I really believe Macready cannot help being as odious as he is on stage. He very nearly
made me faint last night in *Macbeth* with crushing my already broken finger, and, by
way of apology, merely coolly observed that he really could not answer for himself in
such a scene, and that I ought to wear a splint; and truly, if I act more with him, I think
I shall require several splints, for several bones.

Fanny Kemble *(letters to Harriet St Leger, 1848)*

False face must hide what
the false heart doth know.
ACT 1, SCENE 7.

A woman was watching Alec Guinness play *Macbeth* at the Royal Court, when she leant
across to her companion and said very loudly, 'You see how one lie leads to another!'

None but he, whose being I do fear.
ACT 3, SCENE 1.

One evening as Sir Lewis Casson was staring into the gloom with, 'Is this a dagger
which I see before me?' a rather shrill Welsh lady, sitting in the stalls, was heard to
whisper: 'Now look what's happening to him, e's seeing things!'

The night has been unruly ...
ACT 2, SCENE 3.

Sadler's Wells in the 1840s was a squalid bear garden, patronized by thieves and prostitutes. Performances were often interrupted by fights, which would erupt dangerously throughout different parts of the theatre. It was most certainly a place where no respectable person would dare be seen. In order to save the theatre from this den of iniquity, Phelps ordered that the various ringleaders of this rabble should be cleared from the premises. This in turn brought hideous revenge. Charles Dickens attended Samuel Phelp's opening night of Macbeth at Sadler's Wells, 1844.

It was performed amidst the usual hideous medley of fights, foul language, catcalls, shrieks, howls, oaths, blasphemy, obscenity, apples, oranges, nuts, biscuits, ginger beer, porter and pipes. Cans of beer with a pint measure to drink from, were carried through the dense crowd at all stages of the tragedy. Sickly children in arms were squeezed out of shape in all parts of the house. Fish was fried at the entrance doors and barricades of oyster shells encumbered the pavement.

A few years later there was a production of Macbeth *performed at Sadler's Wells, where a different actor played the Thane in each act – the novelty soon wore off.*

Why do you make such faces?
ACT 3, SCENE 4.

Garrick's performance so frightened George III that he never went to see him again.

Macbeth was a role where rapid changes of facial expression were needed. The start on seeing the visionary dagger, for example, was accompanied by an extraordinary sense of real seeing on my face, which affected even those on the stage with me; like the murder of Duncan for example. When this is committed Macbeth's ambition is engulfed by the appalling horror of the deed. One evening when I said to the murderer in the banquet scene, 'There's blood upon thy face', the poor actor was so taken aback by the intensity of this look that he put his hand up to his face and cried, 'Is there, by God! Where?'

David Garrick.

With things forgotten...
ACT 1, SCENE 3.

Bernard Miles tells the story of a tolerant stagehand that once had to take over the part of King Duncan. The young man had been well coached in his lines and got through the opening scenes. However, when they came to Duncan's entry as Macbeth's honoured guest, with the King's courteous greeting to his host, 'This castle hath a pleasant seat; the air nimbly and sweetly recommends itself unto our gentle senses,' memory failed the poor man. He filled in bravely, getting the sense if not the words:

You've got a lovely place 'ere, guvnor.'

Marshall'st me the way that I was going.
ACT 2, SCENE 1.

One Brisco, the manager of a small theatrical company in Staffordshire, though stone blind, last night played a powerful Macbeth. He was ably supported upon the arm of his good lady wife.

Wolverhampton Chronicle. 1767

I think, but dare not speak
ACT 5, SCENE 1

I can recall an occasion while playing Macbeth, when old Barry was in charge. One evening I dried-up in the middle of the dagger speech and anxiously looked towards the wings for help. But old Barry was engaged in some other business at the time and his thoughts were far away. In desperation I called out, 'Barry, give me the line, will you?' To which the old fellow, with the imperturbability of a prompter, and the exquisite unconsciousness of an Irishman, replied, loud enough for all the house to hear; 'All in good time, my boy, all in good time.' He then coolly wet his thumb, turned over a few leaves of the script, and said; 'Now, what line would it be that you after.'

David Garrick

I should report that which I say I saw, But know not how to do't.
ACT 5, SCENE 5.

There was chaos on the one-way system outside Dunsinane today when a large wood appeared out of nowhere. The wood had been transplanted and carried by the invading army of Macduff and Malcolm.

'We wanted to disguise ourselves,' said a large tree, which later turned out to be Malcolm. 'So we thought we would carry a bit of foliage.'

'Let's face it, it's not much of a disguise is it?' said one soldier who had carried a rather well established sycamore for hundreds of miles. 'I mean, the purpose of disguise is not to let the enemy know you're there. He looks out one morning and suddenly sees a huge forest in his front garden, he's bound to be a bit suspicious.'

Nick Page. *The Tabloid Shakespeare.*

The attempt and not the deed confounds us.

ACT 2, SCENE 2.

In 1885, Sir Frank Benson was asked to perform Macbeth at the Cheltenham Ladies' College. The headmistress, Miss Beale, although willing to let her pupils have the benefit of a Shakespeare play in action, felt compelled to protect them from the unhealthy lure of the theatre. There would be no scenery, no furniture and no make-up. The men would wear evening dress. If the words 'God' or 'Hell' appeared in the text, 'Heaven' or 'below' were to be substituted. Moreover, the company was not to look at the audience, which consisted entirely of girls, with one clergyman in the middle of the front row, and no one must laugh on pain of instant execution.

The witches, in full evening dress, walked solemnly round a chair while discussing swine killing, sieve sailing, and pilot's thumbs. Final horror came during the sleepwalking scene. Just as Janet Achurch was in full flight with 'All the perfumes of Arabia will not sweeten this little hand,' Miss Beale walked on to the stage and announced imperiously, 'Pray would you mind waiting a few minutes, I must light the gas.'

J.C. Trewin. *Benson and the Bensonians.* 1960.

Give me some wine; fill full!

ACT 3, SCENE 4.

One evening when Mrs. Siddons was performing Lady Macbeth, she was tempted by a torturing thirst. Her dresser, therefore, dispatched a boy in great haste to 'fetch a pint of beer for Mrs. Siddons.' Meanwhile the play proceeded. When the boy returned with the pint he enquired where he should find Mrs. Siddons, and on being told she was in the middle of the sleep-walking scene, promptly walked on to the stage, tapped Mrs. Siddons on the shoulder and presented her with the beer! Her distress may be imagined; she desperately waved the boy away in her grand manner several times, 'Out, damned spot, out I say,' but without effect. The audience was in an uproar of laughter, which even the dignity of so great an actress as Mrs. Siddons was unable to quell for several minutes.

Thomas Campbell

Adder's fork, and blind-worm's sting
ACT 4, SCENE 1.

You managed to play the first act of my little comedy tonight with all the Chinese flair and light-hearted brilliance of Lady Macbeth.

Noël Coward

Vivien Leigh's Lady Macbeth is more niminy-piminy than thundery-blundery, more viper than anaconda, but still quite competent in its small way.

Kenneth Tynan

Mrs Patrick Campbell twittered through the part and pecked at it like a canary trying to eat a cocoa nut.

William Archer

As Lady Macbeth, Mrs Pat looked like the Queen of Hearts about to have the gardeners executed.

John Gielgud

Flora Robson should flick Lady M. through her soul faster than thought.

James Bridie

Miss Peg Woffington's Lady Macbeth was extremely well received, and did the part as well as her deplorable tragedy voice would admit.

Francis Gentleman

The devil himself could not pronounce a title more hateful to mine ear.

ACT 5, SCENE 6.

In 1749, David Garrick became joint-manager of the Theatre Royal Drury Lane. When this was announced, James Quin enquired of Garrick if he'd considered a good rousing play for the opening season.

'I have indeed, Mr. Quin, sir. I shall open with, *Macbeth* – as written by William Shakespeare, that is.'

'What d'you mean?' retorted Quin. 'Don't I play Macbeth as written by Shakespeare? Why, of course I do.'

'Is that so?' replied Garrick. 'Then the devil damn thee black, thou cream fac'd loon, Where got'st thou that goose look?'

Quin stared at him in horror. 'And who, pray, could conceive of such a remark as that?'

'William Shakespeare, sir! Act 5, Scene 3. Line eleven.

'Absolute, pish!' snorted Quin.

Clive Francis. *An Actor Without Rival to Shine.*

These juggling fiends no more believed

ACT 5, SCENE 6

The approach of death showed each instant on Garrick's face. His plight made the audience shudder, he clawed the ground and seemed to be digging his own grave, but the dread moment was nigh, one saw death in reality, everything expressed that instant which makes all equal ... his eyes became dim, his voice could not support the efforts he made to speak his thoughts. The death rattle and the convulsive movements of the features, arms and breast, gave the final touch to this terrible picture.

Jean Georges Noverre 1760

Garrick wrote a special death speech for himself at the end of the play.

'Tis done! The scene of my life will quickly close!
Ambition's vain delusive dreams are fled
And now I wake in darkness and guilt.
I cannot bear it! Let me shake it off -
'Twa' not be; my soul is clogged with blood.
I cannot rise! I dare not ask for mercy.
It is too late, hell drags me down. I sink,
I sink - Oh! my soul is lost forever!
Oh! (Dies)

Creeps in this petty pace ...
ACT 5, SCENE 5.

As Macbeth, Garrick out-did his usual out-doings.

Colley Cibber

When Ralph Richardson appeared in Gielgud's ill-fated production, he wore a red wig, having sent his wig-maker into the stalls during a matinee of ' The Tempest' to snip a lock of schoolgirl's hair he decided was just the right shade.

Saucy doubts and fears.

ACT 3, SCENE 4.

When Paul Eddington was struggling with his own performance at the Bristol Old Vic, in 1961, he remembers one speech, that used to elude him nightly.

So I put a notice on the company notice board: 'If I do not get through that speech tonight without fluffing or drying I shall clean the boots of the entire company.' My courtiers and cabinet looked at me with eager expectation that night. 'Yes, you buggers,' I thought. 'You're not listening to a word I'm saying about kingship and democracy. You're lining up your boots!' I was damned if I would clean them. It broke a jinx, and I did not have to.

Paul Eddington. *So Far, So Good.*

A poor player
That struts and frets his hour upon the stage

ACT 5, SCENE 5.

Kenneth Tynan summed up Richardson's Macbeth as ...

A sad facsimile of the cowardly lion in The Wizard of Oz ... he moved dully, as if by numbers, and such charm as he possessed was merely a sort of unfocused bluffness, like a teddy-bear snapped in a bad light by a child holding its first camera.

His Macbeth is slovenly; and to go further into it would be as frustrating as trying to write with a pencil whose point has long since worn down to the wood.

Richardson himself was known to be unhappy with his own performance:

One night after delivering the great dagger speech Richardson came over to Raymond Westwell, who was playing Macduff and said, 'Give me five pounds.' Westwell, looked at him in astonishment, 'But why, Ralph?'

'Listen, if you don't give me five pounds, cocky, I'll put it about that you played Macduff to my Macbeth.'

Bloody instructions, which, being taught, return to plague the inventor.

ACT 1, SCENE 7.

In 1980, Peter O'Toole played Macbeth at the Old Vic. Two weeks before rehearsals began, while driving to Connemara to meet his Lady M. (Frances Tomelty) O'Toole's car suddenly went out of control, crashing into a stone wall. As he sat stunned at the wheel, the vehicle began to veer slowly towards the cliff edge. It was Friday 13th. From then on things began to go steadily down hill for the production, becoming one of most notorious in recent years.

After a series of sackings and rows, O'Toole insisted on having the production designed by an eccentric Mexican, whom he referred to as 'the inventor.' He was paid £2,000 and given access to a large rehearsal room where 'the inventor' spent many long hours working on his designs. After two weeks he invited everyone to a demonstration. They were shown a set made out of a series of black bin liners that had been carefully taped together to represent battlements. The bags were lit from inside by tiny light bulbs that had been screwed into tomato juice cans and powered by a loud petrol motor. The noise was so deafening that no one could hear themselves speak. When the demonstration eventually came to an end, there was a deafening silence as the assembled company stared in open horror. O'Toole took immediate action. Dragging on a sagging Gauloise he had the inventor plus bin liners escorted to the Waterloo Road, where he was told never to return. Undeterred, the Mexican returned a little while later – now the worse for drink – and gallantly informed the assembled company, that he didn't give a toss what they thought and that as far as he was concerned they were nothing but a crowd of wankers!

When have you ever heard a critic come out of *Macbeth*, claiming that his sides ached with laughter?

Jack Tinker, *Daily Mail,* 1980

Peter O'Toole delivers every line with a monotonous bark as if addressing
an audience of Eskimos.
Michael Billington.

Remove the means of all annoyance
ACT 5, SCENE 1.

One night while John Philip Kemble was performing Macbeth, he was much interrupted, from time to time, by the squalling of a young child in one of the galleries. At length, angered by this rival performance, Kemble walked with solemn step to the front of the stage, and addressed the audience in his most tragic tones: 'Ladies and gentlemen, unless the play is stopped, the child cannot possibly continue.'

Thomas Moore. *Memoirs, Journals and Correspondence* (1853-56)

It was announced on one occasion at Drury Lane, that 'Four Kings' would attend a performance of *Macbeth*; these in fact were American Indian Chiefs to whom the courtesy title of 'Kings' had been applied. The theatre was correspondingly packed that night ' to see the Kings' who were placed in the centre box. Here they were invisible to the occupants of the gallery, who loudly demanded their money back unless they could see the distinguished visitors. After some haggling with the audience, the manager finally placed four chairs on the stage and the Indian 'Kings' gravely descended from their box to a chorus of loud cheers.

When Robert Elliston took over Drury lane in 1809 he presented an adaptation of *Macbeth* as a burletta – 'A Ballet of Music and Action' is how described it. The production was a mixture of mime, dance, opera and spectacle. There was a special *pas de trios* for the three witches, although he used sixteen witches for the coven scenes. Hecate descended from the clouds, while the ghost of Banquo ascended and descended, wreathed in clouds, through a trapdoor in the stage. Whether it was the result of this last effect or not, at one performance the audience called enthusiastically for Banquo, but the actor had gone home. The audience, however, was insistent on congratulating him in person, so a boy was dispatched to his home to bring him back to the theatre. When, finally, he appeared on the stage, in his own clothes, the audience fell silent, not recognising him. Finally someone in the gallery called out, 'Who's that?' and was answered by a voice in the pit, 'Why, you fool, that's the author!'

James Roose-Evans. *London Theatre.*

Blow the horrid deed in every eye.
ACT 1, SCENE 7.

I once saw Grimaldi, on a benefit night, give the dagger speech in *Macbeth*. It was a darkened scene introduced in a pantomime, and he was in his clown's dress. Notwithstanding, a dead silence pervaded the whole house, and I was not the only boy that trembled.

Anon.

Mrs Pritchard acting as Lady Macbeth resemble those sudden flashes of lightning which more accurately discover the horrors of surrounding darkness.

Francis Gentleman

Be not offended ...
ACT 4, SCENE 3.

Coral Browne once met the actress Vivien Merchant at a party and said, 'I hear you're playing Lady Macbeth. What are you going to do with that fucking candle? Take my advice and don't bring it on. I left mine on a sconce offstage. It's more trouble than it's worth.' Vivien Merchant explained that her director wanted her to play Lady M. in a grey wig with a grey face, 'but I don't think it's quite right somehow, do you?' 'I wouldn't play her in a fucking grey wig,' replied Coral. 'When I played the old cow, I played her as a mature woman, but very lonely. My trouble was I had an extremely jealous actor playing Macbeth. He was bitter and upset as I'd got all the notices; one night he pulled my wig off and threw it across the stage. I think the true crux of the matter was that in the first scene I wanted to play Lady M. with a baby glued to my tit. But he wouldn't hear of it. Afraid I'd get the pathos, you see.'

Joe Orton

And munched and munched and munched.
ACT 1, SCENE 3.

DISH OF THE DAY
Ragout Of Newt

Ingredients:
1 eye of newt - peeled
1 toe of frog
Wool of bat - 300 gm
1 dog's tongue
1 goat's gall bladder
Entrails of a small tiger
(available at selected Chinese food suppliers)
2 eggs
A pinch of mandragora
Lizard's leg
Slow-worm's sting
Curry powder (optional)
Nose of a Turk
Lips of a Tartar
Liver of a blaspheming Jew
(omit if cooking for vegetarians)

Preheat a large cauldron. Put all the ingredients into the pre-heated cauldron. Add 2 litres of fetid water from a poisoned well. Stir well and simmer over a low pyre for 4 hours, chanting all the time. Every now and then stop and drool over the pot in a disgusting, semi-senile way.

After three hours, call on Hecate, spirit of the underworld and dark god of all Scottish food, to bless the pot. Simmer gently for another 10 minutes. Cool the mixture with baboon's blood. Serve with bashed neeps and plenty of shortbread.

This recipe tastes appalling, but will give you the ability to sink ships thousands of miles away.

Nick Page, *The Tabloid Shakespeare*

What are these, so withered and so wild ...?
ACT 1, SCENE 3.

Margaret Webster once had to deputize, at ten minutes notice, for one of the witches who had forgotten there was a matinee. Just before the curtain went up she rushed to the prompt corner and anxiously asked, 'Please wait one minute, which witch am I supposed to be?'

Which Witch?

It is many a year since I launched my career in Shakespeare.
At a most tender age I tottered on stage as a page.
I acted with Tree in – now when would it be?
Eighty-three.
And though it sounds queer in the following year I played Lear.

Ah those were days! And I thought they had gone.
But, during the war, a young man called John
(I think it was Gielgud; I'm not really sure)
Rang me up and invited me out on a tour
For eighty-nine weeks as a witch in *Macbeth* –
A prospect, I thought, little better than death.
But as I'd grown tired of just giving auditions,
I said I would do it, on certain conditions.
I said, 'Mr Gielgud, my dear,
There is one point on which I'm not clear.
We've fixed up the sordid finance, so to speak,
And finally settled on £4 a week,
But in which part am I to appear?

Which witch?
Is it First Witch, or Second, or which?
As one who's played Lady Macbeth in her day,
I must be the witch with the most lines to say.
The tall, scraggy thin one does not int'rest me:
I must be the hag with the gag in Act Three.

If it's the First Witch, my dear, I should love it;
But if it's the Second, you know where you can shove it.
I will not be the one who just croaks in the shade:
I must have the spots on my face, I'm afraid.
To avoid any last-minute hitch,
Would you kindly inform me – which witch?

Don't think I insist on a part that is huge,
But I've never in 69 years, been a stooge.
The part must be one in which I'll get my teeth –
Not the hag who just keeps shouting 'All Hail!' on the heath.
When we're grouped round the cauldron and watching it bubble,
I must be well lit – or else there'll be trouble
We can fix up these things when we start to rehearse
But I must be the witch who has got the best curse.

So, before I pack one single bag
I must know in advance, John – which hag?
It would save some expense if you didn't have three:
Why not lump them together and only have me?

When I'd done, Johnnie G. said, 'Blast!
I will not have that witch in the cast.'
And then I discovered he screamed I'm a bitch.
So I never discovered which witch!

Sung by Hermione Gingold from Sky High, Phoenix Theatre. 1942.
Words by Alan Melville. Music by Charles Zwar.

Let's briefly put on manly readiness.
ACT 2, SCENE 3.

Alec Guinness on his school production in Eastbourne, 1928.

I made a great hit in *Macbeth* as the messenger because I took the precaution of running three times round the playground before I made my entrance so that I could deliver the news in a state of exhaustion.

Infirm of purpose ...

ACT 2, SCENE 2

There was once a production where, as *Macbeth* was carrying out the bloodstained daggers after killing the king, the blades fell off. He stared at them in horror for a moment and then Lady Macbeth, thinking she was saving the situation, swept magnificently across stage and amended her next line to: 'Infirm of purpose! Give me the handles!'

Michael Green. *The Art of Coarse Acting.*

If thou speak'st false ...

ACT 5, SCENE 5

The actor playing Seyton in Donald Wolfit's production had become bored of rushing on every night and informing *Macbeth* that the Queen was dead, and had asked for a larger part. Wolfit refused, and was so angry at his impudence that he sacked the lad just before a performance. When the about-to-be-unemployed actor arrived that evening to deliver the tragic news, he got his revenge on Wolfit by reporting loudly, "The queen, my lord, is much better, and is even now at supper."

Let's make haste; she'll soon be back again.

ACT 3, SCENE 5

Then there was the story of a rather down-and-out actress, who was very out of work, extremely hard up and in desperate need of a job. She had recently been in Beerbohm Tree's company so thought it best to appeal to him.

'Please, Mr. Tree, give me something. You know what I can do. I can do anything, anything, from Lady Macbeth to the cloakroom woman.'

'My dear woman,' replied Tree. 'We already have a Lady Macbeth and she is the cloakroom woman.'

O valiant cousin!

ACT 1, SCENE 2.

With hair swept back like Toshiro Mifune in a Samurai epic and poker-back stance, Ian McKellen is at first your perfect soldier. But when he talks of his 'single state of man' being shaken, his body gives an involuntary shudder. If this is not great acting, I don't know what is.

Michael Billington.

I'll devil-porter it no further.

ACT 2, SCENE 3

In 1975, Judi Dench and Ian McKellen played the Macbeths in a memorable production at Stratford's little theatre, The Other Place, directed by Trevor Nunn. The critics were unstinting in their praise and heralded the production as one of the most remarkable in recent years. Robert Cushman, in the Observer, *said Judi Dench's performance '… edges her ring of confidence with steel; murder, as she counsels it, sounds the most sensible thing in the world.'*

Ian McKellen remembers the occasion:

Our *Macbeth* wasn't set in Scotland; it took place in the theatre. The cast of twelve sat round in a magic circle of beer crates, on a plain wooden floor, from where they watched the scenes they weren't part of. The sound effects were openly made by the actors. My first job was to rattle the thundersheet as the doors of the theatre were banged shut.

John Napier's entire set cost £200, and the costumes were a ragbag of second-hand clothes. My uniform jacket had buttons embossed with 'Birmingham Fire Service,' and Judi Dench wore a dyed tea-towel on her head. Somehow it was magic: and black magic, too. A priest used to sit on the front row, whenever he could scrounge a ticket, holding out his crucifix to protect the cast from the evil we were raising.

There was so much I was proud of with the production: discovering how to play a soliloquy direct into the eyes of everyone in the audience; making them laugh at *Macbeth*'s gallows humour; and, over all, working alongside Judi Dench's finest performance.

Ian McKellen *Acting Shakespeare*

When the production transferred to the Old Vic, a few months earlier, an incident took place, which misplaced the story completely. One night the theatre intercom got caught up with a local taxi service. Just as Lady Macbeth was saying, 'Pray you, keep seat; the fit is momentary' the audience were entertained with, 'Two for Basingstoke, when you're ready Fred!'

We will proceed no further in this business.

ACT 1, SCENE 7

James Agate remembers Charles Laughton's Macbeth at the Old Vic in 1933
At the words 'Avaunt, and quit my sight!' Laughton bounced from the ghost landing half-way up the staircase like an India-rubber cat.

Laughton had a miserable first night, and sat slumped in his chair, no one daring to enter his room. Suddenly Lilian Baylis stormed in and slapped him hard on the back. 'Never mind, dear, you did your best, and one day I expect you'll make quite a good Macbeth.'

Be not a niggard of your speech.
ACT 4, SCENE 3.

Flora Robson's Lady M. did not fare better at the hands of Mr Agate, either.
I am not as yet convinced that this fiercely intelligent and finely emotional actress is
entitled to be called a tragedienne. If she is, then I submit that the tragedy of *Macbeth*
is of Dryden's colour and not Shakespeare.

The following night she received a letter from the playwright, James Bridie

> My dear Flora,
> I didn't come back-stage because I was genuinely
> heart-broken. It's no use lying about it, I thought your
> Lady Macbeth wrong, wrong, wrong; lifeless, inept,
> even stupid ... you acted [her] like a schoolgirl in love
> with her head-mistress ... when you said the Raven
> itself was hoarse, I expected you to follow it up by
> saying that when you'd got Duncan's spare room
> ready, you'd go up and rub the bird with Sloane's
> liniment.

An American couple was watching John Clements's performance from the front stalls at
Chichester, 1966. It was a Thursday evening, and when he got to the soliloquy,
'Tomorrow and tomorrow and tomorrow ...' the husband turned eagerly to his wife;
'Did you get that Honey? That means Sunday.'

One afternoon at the opera an American was over-heard to say, 'I thought Shakespeare
wrote *Macbeth*.' 'He did dear,' said his wife. 'Then who the hell's this guy Verdi.'

Deny me this and an eternal curse fall on you!

Simone Signoret simply can't speak the verse and that's that.
Went round and told her she was marvellous.
Kenneth Williams. *The Diaries.*

Be not lost so poorly in your thoughts.
ACT 2, SCENE 2.

Simone Signoret played Lady Macbeth, opposite Alec Guinness,
at the Royal Court Theatre in 1966.

On the third evening the last reviews had fallen before mine eyes – or rather on my head – just before I went onstage. There wasn't a reason in the world, I thought, that everyone in the audience hadn't read them too. And so it so happened that during my first scene with Alec Guinness, during my third or fourth speech, I suddenly stopped. He caught on and saved me. He slid in, 'If we should fail ...' which comes much later in the scene. He used it to save his friend, who was in the process of drowning, having 'dried up.' It helped me to go on, and since we were playing to an audience of connoisseurs, they applauded.

Simone Signoret. *Nostalgia Ain't What It Used To Be.*

Strange garments, cleave not to their mould
ACT 1, SCENE 3

Simone Signoret's Lady Macbeth, a conical, bell-tented matron who moves
about on wheels like a draped Dalek.

Alan Brien. *Sunday Telegraph,* 1966

Michael Hordern played Macbeth at the Old Vic, opposite Beatrice Lehmann, in 1959. The press were most unkind, accusing Hordern of imposing comedy on the play where none existed or was intended.

Michael Hordern as Macbeth is ludicrously costumed. He spends half the time on stage cringed like an Armenian carpet seller in an ankle-length black dressing gown of fuzzy candlewick, while his ruched sleeves sag like concertinas around the tips of his sleeves ... This Thane of Cawdor would be unnerved by Banquo's valet, never mind Banquo's ghost.

She has spoke what she should not.

ACT 5, SCENE 1.

In The Macbeth Murder Mystery, *by James Thurber, an English lady whilst on holiday in the Lakes, meets up with an American lady, who happens to be a great lover of detective stories. Disappointingly all she can find to read in her hotel bedroom is* Macbeth.

'Tell me,' I said. 'did you read *Macbeth*?'

'I had to,' she said. 'There wasn't a scrap of anything else to read in the whole room.'

'Did you like it?' I asked.

'No, I did not,' she said decisively. 'In the first place, I don't think for a moment that he killed the King. I don't think that Macbeth woman was mixed up in it, either. You suspect them the most, of course, but those are the ones that are never guilty – or shouldn't be, anyway.'

I thought this over while I filled my pipe. 'Who do you suspect?' I asked, suddenly.

'Macduff,' she said, promptly.

'Good God!' I whispered, softly.

'Oh, Macduff did it, all right. At first I suspected Banquo. And then, of course, he was the second person killed. The person you suspect of the first murder should always be the second victim.'

'Is that so?' I murmured.

'Oh, yes,' said my informant. 'They have to keep surprising you. Well, after the second murder I didn't know who the killer was for a while.'

'How about Malcolm and Donalbain, the King's sons?' I asked. 'As I remember it, they fled right after the first murder. That looks suspicious.'

'Too suspicious,' said the American lady. 'Much too suspicious. When they flee, they're never guilty. You can count on that.'

'I believe, I'll have a brandy,' and I summoned the waiter.

'But what do you make of the Third Murderer?' I asked. 'You know, the Third Murderer has puzzled *Macbeth* scholars for three hundred years.'

'That's because they never thought of Macduff, ' said the American lady. 'It was Macduff, I'm certain. You couldn't have one of the victims murdered by two ordinary thugs – the murderer always has to be somebody important.'

'But what about the banquet scene?' I asked, after a moment. 'How do you account for Macbeth's guilty actions there, when Banquo's ghost came in and sat in his chair?'

The lady leaned forward and tapped me on the knee. 'There wasn't any ghost,' she said. 'A big, strong man like that doesn't go around seeing ghosts – especially in a brightly lighted banquet hall with dozens of people around. Macbeth was shielding somebody!'

'Who was he shielding?' I asked.

'Mrs Macbeth, of course,' she said.

'But what about the sleep-walking scene, then?'

'The same thing, only the other way round,' said my companion. 'That time she was shielding him. She wasn't asleep at all. Do you remember where it says, "Enter Lady Macbeth with a taper"?'

'Yes,' I said.

'Well, people who walk in their sleep never carry lights! They have a second sight. Did you ever hear of a sleepwalker carrying a light?'

'No,' I said, 'I never did.'

'Well, then, she wasn't asleep. She was acting guilty to shield Macbeth.'

'I think,' I said, 'I'll have another brandy,' and I called the waiter. 'I believe that you have got hold of something. Would you lend me that *Macbeth*? I'd like to look it over tonight. I don't feel, somehow, as if I'd ever really read it.'

'I'll get it for you,' she said. 'But you'll find that I am right.'

James Thurber. *The Great Macbeth Mystery*

The great Italian actor Tommaso Salvini thought, and even printed, that the sleep-walking scene must have been written for *Macbeth*, and then stolen from him by an unscrupulous actress.

After a performance in Edinburgh, a theatregoer was heard to remark;

'Don't you think Lady Macbeth puts you mind of Mrs McAndrew? She had something of the same problem you know.'

The Night I Appeared as Macbeth

'The Night I Appeared as Macbeth', was a famous musical hall song of the 1920s and parodied the time-honoured practice of 'improving' on the Bard.

'Twas thro' a Y.M.C.A. concert
I craved a desire for the stage.
In Wigan one night, I was asked to recite,
Gadzooks, I was quickly the rage.
They said I was better than Irving,
And gave me some biscuits and tea,
I know it's not Union wages,
But that was the usual fee.
Home I came, bought some dress,
Appeared in your theatre and what a success.

I acted so tragic the house rose like magic,
The audience yelled 'You're sublime!'
They made me a present of Mornington Crescent,
They threw it a brick at a time.
Someone threw a fender which caught me a bender,
I hoisted a white flag and tried to surrender,
They jeered me, they queered me,
And half nearly stoned me to death.
They threw nuts and sultanas, fried eggs and bananas
The night I appeared as *Macbeth*.

The advertised time for the curtain
Was six forty-five on the sheet.
The hall keeper he having mislaid the key,
We played the first act in the street.
Then somebody called for the author,
'He's dead' said the flute-player's wife –
The news caused an awful commotion,
And gave me the shock of my life.
Shakespeare dead, dear old Bill,
Why I never knew the poor fellow was ill.

I acted so tragic the house rose like magic,
They wished David Garrick could see.
But he's in the Abbey, then someone quite shabby
Suggested that's where I should be.
I withdrew my sabre, and started to labour,
Cried 'Lay on Macduff' to my swashbuckle neighbour,
I hollered 'I'm collared, and I must
Reach the bridge or it's death!'
But they altered my journey, I reached the infirm'ry
The night I appeared as Macbeth.

William Hargreaves. (1922)

We have scorched the snake, not killed it...

ACT 3, SCENE 2.

One afternoon a leading critic [James Agate] bustled into my dressing-room, halfway through the matinee performance. I had met him once or twice before this time, but naturally I was never very much at ease in his august presence.

He began by saying that he had dragged himself to the theatre, full of the direst presentiments: that I should fail as Macbeth had seemed a foregone conclusion to him. He then remarked: 'I have never seen the Murder Scene better done, and so I have come to congratulate you now. At the end of the performance I shall probably have changed my mind, for you can't possibly play the rest of it.' I murmured my thanks, and he went back to his seat. All through the second half of the play I was acutely self-conscious. I felt sure that I was over-acting every scene. I was amazed to read a favourable notice in his column the following Sunday, one of the most favourable, in fact, that he has ever given me.

John Gielgud

I never feel at ease when a critic comes to my dressing room. Critics, like clergymen, always seem out of place behind the scenes.

John Gielgud.

When Gielgud said he was planning to do Macbeth, Alexander Woollcott told him that the Lunts [Lynn Fontaine and Alfred Lunt] had always wanted to produce the play.

'**L**ynn has a wonderful idea,' he said. 'She will go naked to murder Duncan.' Gielgud agreed this would be a sensational effect, but how did she propose to do it? 'Oh,' said Woollcott, 'there will be a very high parapet between her and the audience; she will keep her pudenda strictly for Alfred.'

Good sir, why do you start, and seem to fear ...?

ACT 1, SCENE 3.

In 1929, Gielgud played Macbeth at the Old Vic

My physical picture of the character was derived principally from the drawings of Henry Irving by Bernard Partridge.

John Gielgud

Double, double, toil and trouble ...

ACT 4, SCENE 1.

Kitty Black, who was working for the producers H.M.Tennent, remembers Gielgud's production at the Piccadilly Theatre, in 1942.

For a long time John couldn't make up his mind about the Lady, and finally announced that he would hold auditions in order to find a suitable new star. Among the letters was one application for the part of 'Lady McBeth' enclosing a photograph with the pathetic p.s. 'I do take my glasses off often.' From the first the disasters that seem to dog the Scottish play began to accumulate. First, William Walton disappeared. His agent had no idea where he was and as the music he had commissioned to write had been conceived as an accompaniment to all the witches' scenes, which were to be spoken rhythmically against a recorded score, nobody could rehearse anything final until the composer had set down what had been agreed with the director. One day the office boy came into my room saying: 'There's a bloke outside who says he's supposed to be composing the music for *Macbeth*.'

'Mr. Walton, Mr. Walton,' I cried, hurrying out to meet him, 'where have you been? Where's the music?'

'I haven't written it yet,' he replied.

'Not written it!' I gasped. 'But we need it right away.'

'It won't take long,' he replied and proceeded to explain that composing the twenty-odd minutes of music required would barely take him a week, and he was as good as his word. He attended only one run-through of the play, made careful notes and when the score was delivered, every fanfare and musical bridge was correctly timed to the very last second.

John had [also] put together a tremendously complicated effects score with wind howling at all the climaxes, bells ringing, doors being hammered on, etc, and the only way all this could be co-ordinated was for two operators – Mary and Viola – to manipulate the gramophones with pick-up arms that could be spotted on to any given groove of the 78s – with the effects on one machine and the Walton music on the other. John kept changing his mind and adding or subtracting effects with the result that finally there were one hundred and forty separate cues for effects, while the music was fed in to compliment or underline the action. After the final matinee, John came up to

Viola and asked her to add another wind cue to the plot.

'But, Mr. Gielgud, there's only one more performance,' wailed the harassed stage-manager.

'Yes, I know, but I would like to hear it just once,' said John, and who could resist him.

Kitty Black. *Upper Circle.* 1984

You secret, black, and midnight hags!
ACT 4, SCENE 1

Sir Herbert Beerbohm Tree once contemplated a production of *Macbeth* with the idea of casting the 'black hags' literally black. A few candidates turned up in the flesh, and one replied by letter:

> Dear Sir,
> I hear you are looking for dark people.
>   I would like to see you.
>
> Signed Sardanapulus.
> *P.S. I can lift a grand piano with my teeth.*

'Tis better thee without than he within ...
ACT 3, SCENE 4.

A critic once asked Beerbohm Tree why he was considering a silent movie of *Macbeth*.
'I thought I'd reached that time of life, when it's best
to be seen, but not heard!'

I'll charm the air to give a sound ...
ACT 4, SCENE 1

Although Henry Irving was knighted for his magnificent services to the theatre, Sarah Bernhardt thought him nothing more than 'mediocre.' Bernard Shaw found him hard to take seriously as well, refusing to attend his funeral service in Westminster Abbey. 'Irving would turn in his coffin if I came,' remarked Shaw, 'just as Shakespeare will turn in his coffin when Irving comes.' Nevertheless, Sir Henry played Macbeth at the Lyceum Theatre in 1833.

Those who saw Irving at his best know that today none stands in such lonely splendour. Greatest when he had assistance from the greatest; recall *Macbeth*, Act 1, scene 5. Ellen Terry seated in huge high-backed chair, loose-robed in peacock blue, shimmering silver ornaments in fair hair – every inch a queen of the stage – reading a letter, each syllable dropping clear as water from an icicle. Fiercely she seizes Opportunity, no milk of human kindness in her, clutches at her breasts under the blue robe, furiously appeals to hell for aid, grasps at the murdering dagger, cries 'Hold, hold...,' Suddenly enter from behind the arras ... *Macbeth*, 'Great Glamis!' Recall how Irving paused to stare in wonder, as she, exulting, embraces him and murmurs, 'Great Glamis! worthy Cawdor!' (What an entrance, nothing in all the entrances in all the plays excels it.) Then in four lines she tells him her intent ... They were always very careful about entrances. Recall Act 1, Scene 7, Irving ending his soliloquy, almost in tears, voice trembling, sorry for himself ... Terry rushes in from doorway lower R ... He turns on her terrified. 'What news?' he gasps, struggling to smile, and again she sweeps him into the flooding tide of her iniquity. In that brief scene every phase of human emotion came from their voices, gestures. He self-centred, reluctant to risk. She, annoyed, bitter, sarcastic, contemptuous. He sulky, turns back on her. She works herself up into a fury, dashes hands against the battlements. He gives way. Her 'we fail' – the splendid scorn in her cry. Irving shouts admiration, wonder, his eyes dilated, whole body quivering with homage for such a wife. At the curtain I remember Gladstone in a box, hand behind ear, intent with admiration, rising to applaud with the whole house, gloriously rejoicing.

James Agate. *Part of a letter from Los Angeles.*

Irving once asked his dresser, Walter Collinson, what he thought was his best part.
After much thought he said, 'Macbeth.'
'Really,' said Irving. 'It is generally conceded to be Hamlet.'
'Oh, no, sir, Macbeth. You sweat twice as much in that.'

Macbeth is ripe for shaking.
Act 4, Scene 3

The king is going to visit
The castle of Macbeth;
His hostess sees the way it goes
And plots the monarch's death.

O mucky is the murder,
And bloody is the spot!
Macbeth can scarcely say his prayers,
Which bothers him a lot.

O grisly are the goings-on,
And Lady M's a scold!
But Macbeth's King; and that's the thing
The ancient hags foretold.

They also said that Banquo
Would sire a line of kings;
So Macbeth adds his murder
To all the other things.

They've barely laid the table
To celebrate the feat
When Banquo's ghost upsets his host
By sitting down to eat.

They've barely had the starters
And sung a little toast
When everyone runs off in fear
To see a hungry ghost.

The witches now are stirring
A cauldron in a cave;
Here comes Macbeth to ask of them
How he must now behave

They tell him to beware Macduff;
That done, he's safe to reign
Till Birnam Wood shall up and move
Itself to Dunsinane.

No one who is of woman born
can hurt the wretched man.
Does he not know Macduff's Mama
Had a Caesarean?

Macduff and Malcolm, raising
The standard of the sane,
Advance on Macbeth's castle,
Royal Dunsinane.

They cut the woods of Birnam
To camouflage their way
And, singing lovely choruses,
Embark upon the fray.

O terrible the tyrant's rage,
And hard his Lady's lot!
She walks about in sleep, and cries:
'O damn this bloody spot!'

The Lady dies, Macbeth is killed –
He's not been sharp enough,
For one who's not of woman born
Is obviously Macduff.

Paul Griffin.

Macbeth might be likened to some oak, magnificent in outer shell but lacking roots, and thus riven by the lightning of conscience.

James Agate.

I go, and it is done;
ACT 2, SCENE 1.

Mrs. Siddons took her professional farewell of the stage on, June 29th, 1812. The play was *Macbeth*. At an early hour a vast crowd assembled around the theatre of Covent Garden, and, when the doors were opened, the struggle for places became a service of danger. After the sleepwalking scene, the applause of the spectators became ungovernable: they stood on the benches, and demanded that the performance of the piece should go no further than the last scene in which she appeared. As this wish seemed to be felt by the majority, the actor Chapman came forward, and signified that it should be complied with. And the play ended there.

The night is long that never finds the day.
ACT 4, SCENE 3

Mrs. Siddons describes her reactions to reading Macbeth for the first time.
She wrote in her diary:

I shut myself up as usual, when all the family were retired, and commenced my study of Lady Macbeth. As the character is very short, I thought I should soon accomplish it. With tolerable composure I went on into the silence of the night (a night I never can forget), till I came to the assassination scene, when the horrors of the scene rose to a degree that made it impossible for me to go any farther. I snatched up my candle and hurried out of the room in a paroxysm of terror. My dress was of silk, and the rustling of it, as I ascended the stairs to go to bed, seemed to my panic-struck fancy like the movement of a spectre pursuing me. At last I reached my chamber, where I found my husband fast asleep. I clapt my candlestick down upon the table, without the power of putting the candle out, and threw myself upon the bed without even daring to even to take off my clothes.

Sarah Siddons. *Diaries*

Hence, horrible shadow!

ACT 3, SCENE 4.

One evening in 1945, when Yvonne Mitchell was playing Second Witch at the Bristol Old Vic, she noticed an enormous figure in sand-coloured drapes standing motionless and still, like a statue. When she looked again, it was gone.

Later, she was told that she had seen the ghost of Sarah Siddons and what's more during a performance of *Macbeth*. Apparently she comes to mourn her lost lover who hanged himself there.

Those which have walked in their sleep

ACT 5, SCENE 1.

Diana Wynyard played Lady Macbeth at Stratford, in 1949.

A devotee of the truth, Diana Wynyard insisted on playing the sleepwalking scene with her eyes closed. She had discovered that this was how somnambulists apparently walked – so all during rehearsals she successfully kept her eyes closed, and without incident. Unfortunately, on the opening night, her nerves got the better of her, she walked completely off the end of the set, crashed through a number of ramps, eventually toppling off the parapet altogether, breaking everything in sight – including a number of bones!

Diana Wynyard once said to Noël Coward, 'I saw your *Private Lives* the other night, and didn't laugh once.' Coward replied: 'I saw your Lady Macbeth the other night – and simply roared!'

Confusion now hath made his masterpiece.

Act 2, Scene 3.

Charlton Heston describes in his journals of 1975 the closing night of his Macbeth.

Well I've done the play again. I've climbed the bloody mountain; I've seen the goddamn elephant. Every one of these mother-loving parts is a man-killer, and I've only barely escaped alive from this one each time.

John Gielgud once remarked to Coral Browne that he'd heard that Judi Dench was about to play Lady Macbeth.

'**O**h,' replied Coral, 'then I suppose we shall have the postcard scene.'

Whose horrid image doth unfix my hair ...

ACT 1, SCENE 3.

William Hazlitt describes the way Edmund Kean played the scene after the murder of Duncan. Drury Lane Theatre, November 5th, 1814.

His remorse and terror was amongst the most masterly that the stage has ever witnessed. As a lesson in humanity, it was heartrending. The hesitation, the bewildered look, the coming to himself when he sees his hands bloody; the manner in which his voice clung to his throat, and choked his utterance, his agony and tears, the force of nature overcome by passion – beggared description. It was a scene which no one who saw it can ever efface from his recollection. You cannot say that Kean's Macbeth has style. You can only judge his performance by the number of electric shocks in it.

I'll see no more ...

ACT 4, SCENE 1.

At six years old, Kean, made his stage debut at Drury Lane in 1793, under the name of Carey, when he appeared in a production of Macbeth, with Mrs. Siddons and Kemble.

Kean played one of the evil sprites in attendance on the Three Witches. He played it for one night only. While he and the other sprites stood in line at the mouth of the cave, Edmund slipped and fell against the boy in front, who in turn knocked over the boy in front of him, and so on, until the whole line rolled over like so many toy soldiers. The six-year-old apologized to Kemble, explaining that it was the first time he had appeared in tragedy. Kemble sacked him on the spot!

Champion me to the utterance!

ACT 3, SCENE 1.

Bernard Miles opened his Mermaid Theatre in 1952 with a production of Macbeth spoken entirely in 17th-century English, giving, as Kenneth Tynan suggests, a violent likeness to Stage Rustic and setting the play firmly in that of a farmyard.

Mr. Miles himself embraces the dialect like an old friend (which in his case it is) and goes dourly to work. Gaudy and ostentatious, he struts like a prize rooster, vivid in scarlet and gold. All of which is absolutely faithful to the play; but the poetry, in these accents, rings false, and I realized for the first time why Shakespeare had not bothered to provide death scenes for either Macbeth or his lady. I believe he had stopped liking them, and so, at the Mermaid, did I.

But why stands Macbeth thus amazedly?

ACT 4, SCENE 1.

A bankrupt touring company was once performing *Macbeth* when a man from the Electricity Board came to cut off the supply. The stage-door keeper understanding the urgency of the matter, draped himself in a heavy cloak, put on a large velvet hat and walked on to the stage, right in the middle of the banqueting scene. To the astonishment of the actors he marched up to Macbeth, and said, 'Forgive me, my Lord, but there is one without that, but for us placing upon his palm certain gold pieces within the instant, threateneth to douse yon glim!'

John Mortimer *as told to him by Laurence Olivier.*

Thou marvell'st at my words

ACT 3, SCENE 2.

Michael Meyer remembers playing Scrabble with Graham Greene in Tahiti. Occasionally Greene would come up with some improbable word, usually containing a Z or a Q, the highest scoring letters, claiming it was an Elizabethan obscenity or the like.

One afternoon he claimed 'quoign', which he said was a building term, though he was not sure precisely what. When I queried it, Graham triumphantly quoted what he claimed to be a line from *Macbeth*. 'Yon castle's quoign doth Duncan's spirit haunt' or something of the sort, and when I said this didn't sound like a Shakespeare line to me, he retorted: 'I know I am right, because when I was at school I learned the whole of *Macbeth* by heart.' 'Really?' I asked, and he said: 'Yes, from the first line, "So fair and foul a day I have not seen" to the last, "Whom we invite to see us crowned at Scone".' I said: 'that doesn't impress me. The first line of *Macbeth* is "When shall we three meet again?" ' 'No, that's the second scene. The play begins with Macbeth and Banquo walking across the blasted heath.' 'No, the witches.' Our argument became so heated that we resolved to drive off at once in search of a Shakespeare but [found] only an American paperback unpromisingly entitled *Everything Shakespeare Ever Wrote*, with modernized spelling. We looked up *Macbeth*, and I was proved right about the opening scene, which annoyed Graham; then he tracked down his line, which was not by any means as he had quoted it but did contain the word in the sense of which he had spoken, but spelt 'coin'. This he said was clearly a modernization.

Michael Meyer. *Not Prince Hamlet.*

What you eggs!

ACT 4, SCENE 2.

Apparently someone told Mrs Patrick Campbell that in the sleep-walking scene Lady Macbeth should be seen as through a sheet of glass. On hearing this Bernard Shaw replied: I wish I had been there with a few bricks: there would not have been much left of your glass. Why do you believe every ASS who talks nonsense to you – no: why should I insult the asses – every DOLT!

O well done! I commend your pains.

Act 4, Scene 1

Laurence Olivier and Vivien Leigh
Laurence Olivier – the greatest 'Macbeth' since 'Macbeth.'

Harold Hobson, *1954.*

Take thy face hence!

ACT 5, SCENE 3.

Vivien Leigh on Olivier's entrance as Macbeth at the Old Vic, 1937:
First you hear Macbeth's opening line, then on comes Larry's make-up, followed by Banquo, followed by Larry.

Kenneth Tynan on Olivier's Macbeth, Stratford, 1955.
Last Tuesday Sir Laurence Olivier shook hands with greatness, and within a week or so his performance will have ripened into a masterpiece: not of the superficial, booming, have-a-bash kind, but the real thing, a structure of perfect forethought and proportion, lit by flashes of intuitive lightning ... The needle of Sir Laurence's compass leads him so directly to the heart of the role that we forget the jagged rocks of laughter over which he is travelling ... On the battlements his throttled fury switches into top gear, and we see a lion, baffled but still colossal ... the actor swaying with grief, his voice rising like hair on the crest of a trapped animal.

What bloody man is that?

ACT 1, SCENE 1.

William Macready stumbled off stage one night, only to find that the bowl of blood (cochineal), for him to smear on his hands, had failed to be set. In a blind panic, Macready rushed up to an inoffensive commercial traveller, who was standing in the wings, and without warning, punched him violently on the nose. Blood spurted everywhere. 'Forgive me,' hissed Macready, rinsing his hands under the man's nose, 'but my need is somewhat urgent.'

When the curtain fell Macready presented a five-pound note to the snivelling man, apologizing for any discomfort he may have caused. The commercial traveller tore the money in half, and left. But not before giving Macready a good thumping on the nose as well.

Who's there i'the name of Belzebub?

Act 2, Scene 3.

In 1836 Charles Dickens quite brilliantly caught the manic atmosphere of life backstage, when he described the eccentric behaviour of the cast preparing for a production of
Macbeth.

A quarter before eight – there will be a full house tonight – six parties in the boxes, already; four little boys and a woman in the pit; and two fiddles and a flute in the orchestra, who have got through five overtures since seven o'clock (the hour fixed for the commencement of the performances), and have just begun the sixth. There will be plenty of it, though, when it does begin, for there is enough in the bill to last six hours at least.

The gentleman in the white hat and checked shirt, brown coat and brass buttons, lounging behind the stage-box on the O.P. side, is Mr Horatio St Julien, alias Jem Larkins. His line is genteel comedy – his father's coal and potato. He does Alfred Highflier in the last piece, and very well he'll do it – at the price. The party of gentlemen in the opposite box, to whom he has just nodded, are friends and supporters of Mr Beverley (otherwise Loggins) the Macbeth of the night. The remainder of the audience – a tolerably numerous one by this time – are a motley group of dupes and blackguards ...

The little narrow passages beneath the stage are neither especially clean nor too brilliantly lighted; and the absence of any flooring, together with the damp mildewy smell that pervades the place, does not conduce in any great degree to their comfortable appearance. Don't fall over this basket – it's one of the 'properties' – the cauldron for the witches' cave; and the three uncouth-looking figures, with broken clothes-pegs in their hands, who are drinking gin-and-water out of a pint pot, are the weird sisters. This miserable room, lighted by candles in sconces placed at lengthened intervals round the wall, is the dressing-room, common to the gentlemen performers, and the square hole in the ceiling is the trap-door of the stage above. You will observe that the ceiling is ornamented with the beams that support the boards, and tastefully hung with cobwebs.

The characters in the tragedy are all dressed, and their own clothes are scattered in hurried confusion over the wooden dresser, which surrounds the room. That snuff-shop-looking figure, in front of the glass, is Banquo, and the young lady with the liberal display of legs, who is kindly painting his face with a hare's foot, is dressed for Fleance. The large woman, who is consulting the stage directions in Cumberland's edition of *Macbeth*, is the Lady Macbeth of the night; she is always selected to play the part, because she is tall and stout, and looks a little like Mrs Siddons – at a considerable distance.

The large woman, who is consulting the stage directions,
is the Lady Macbeth of the night.

That stupid-looking milksop, with light hair and bow legs – a kind of man you can warrant town-made – is fresh caught; he plays Malcolm tonight, just to accustom himself with the audience. He will get on better by degrees; he will play Othello in a month, and in a month more, will very probably be apprehended on a charge of embezzlement. The black-eyed female, with whom he is talking so earnestly, is dressed for the 'gentlewoman'. It is her first appearance, too – in the character. The boy of fourteen who is having his eyebrows smeared with soap and whitening, is Duncan, King of Scotland; and the two dirty men with the corked countenances, in very old green tunics, and dirty drab boots, are the 'army.'

'Look sharp below there, gents,' exclaims the dresser, a red-headed and red-whiskered Jew, calling through the trap, 'they're a-going to ring up. The flute says he'll be blowed if he plays any more, and they're getting precious noisy in front.' A general rush immediately takes place to the half-dozen little steep steps leading to the stage, and the heterogeneous groups are soon assembled at the side scenes, in breathless anxiety and motley confusion.

'Now,' cries the manager, consulting the written list, which hangs behind the first P.S. wing. 'Scene 1, open country – lamps down – thunder and lightning – all ready, White?' (This is addressed to one of the army.) 'All ready.' – 'Very well. Scene 2, front chamber. Is the front chamber down?' – 'Yes.' – 'Very well.' – 'Jones' (to the other army who is up in the flies.) 'Hallo!' – 'Wind up the open country when we ring up.' – 'I'll take care.' – 'Scene 3, back perspective with practical bridge. Bridge ready, White? Got the trestles there?' – 'All right.'

'Very well. Clear the stage,' cries the manager, hastily packing every member of the company into the little space there is between the wings and the wall, and one wing and another. 'Places, places. Now then, Witches – Duncan – Malcolm – bleeding officer – where's the bleeding officer?' – 'Here!' replies the officer, who has been rose pinking for the character. 'Get ready, then; now, White, ring the second music-bell.' The actors who are to be discovered are hastily arranged, and the actors who are not to be discovered, place themselves, in their anxiety to peep at the house, just where the audience can see them. The bell rings, and the orchestra, in acknowledgement of the call, play three distinct chords. The bell rings – the tragedy opens – and our description closes.

Charles Dickens. *Sketches by Boz.* 1836.

Fair is foul and foul is fair.

ACT 1, SCENE 1.

The great Samuel Phelps, early in his career, was engaged to play seven characters – all for a guinea a week.

I don't think I distinguished myself very highly. The fact is, I only had one wig for the Witch and Duncan, and as I didn't know much about the art of making up, I couldn't get the beastly stuff off my face in time for all my changes. So there was a family likeness between the weird sister, Duncan, the Physician, and the unfortunate 'cream-faced loon'. I got through the great scene with Macduff and struggled through the Physician with only the occasional break-down in communication, but when I came on as 'first officer' to form part of Macbeth's valiant army in one scene, and then of the 'cream-faced loon' in Macduff's yet more valiant army in another, I got so helplessly mixed up, that I completely 'corpsed' poor Hamilton, our leading man, a great strapping fellow. He laughed so much that his Scotch bonnet brushed against a candelabra – setting fire to the brim of it!

Samuel Phelps. *1868*

Now good digestion wait on appetite.

ACT 3, SCENE 4.

Sir Frank Benson played Macbeth, to the horror of the traditionalists, bare-legged. He was also a hard taskmaster and on one occasion kept his company rehearsing for nearly seven hours without meals. As Macbeth reached the cry, 'They have tied me to a stake!' one actor loudly exclaimed, 'I wish to God they'd tie me to one!'

Fillet of a fenny snake
In the cauldron boil and bake;

ACT 4, SCENE 1

Eye of newt, and toe of frog,
Wool of bat, and tongue of dog,
Adder's fork, and blind-worm's sting,
Lizard's leg and howlet's wing,
Scale of dragon, tooth of wolf,
Witch's mummy, maw and gulf
Of the ravined salt sea shark,
Root of hemlock digged i' the dark,
Liver of blaspheming Jew,
Gall of goat, and slips of yew
Slivered in the moon's eclipse,
Nose of Turk, and Tartar's lips,
Finger of birth-strangled babe,
Ditch-delivered by a drab
Cool it with a baboon's blood
Then the charm is firm and good.

William Shakespeare

Unsex me here ...

ACT 1, SCENE 5.

I could never bring myself to play the part of someone with such curious
notions of hospitality.

Edith Evans *on Lady Macbeth*

To mankind in general, Macbeth and Lady Macbeth stand out as the supreme type of
all that a host and hostess should not be.
Max Beerbohm

Should I stay longer ...?

ACT 4, SCENE 2.

Donald Sinden remembers a production he was in at Stratford in 1946.

Shakespeare's plays are full of stumbling blocks for the unwary actor; *Macbeth* has several, two of them occurring within four lines. The king has been murdered and members of the household are told the terrible news as they arrive. His two sons Malcolm and Donalbain appear and Donalbain asks 'What is amiss?' to be told, 'You are and do not know't.' Macduff then tells them 'Your noble father's murdered,' to which Malcolm replies in a line so apparently offhand that it is fraught with danger, 'O by whom?' Paul Scofield was playing Malcolm and was talking in my dressing room one evening when he missed his call for this scene. We suddenly heard shouts and the sound of running feet: I opened my door and saw an approaching stage-manager shouting, 'Paul! Paul! You're on!' Paul went out of his room like a rocket, leapt down the stairs, arrived breathless on the stage and was informed, 'Your noble father's murdered.' Only when he tried to say 'O ...' did he realized he had a cigarette in his mouth. He removed it, threw it to the floor, ground it with his foot, and continued, 'By whom?' Later it was pointed out that he had also failed to put on his wig.

Donald Sinden. *A Touch of the Memoirs*

Make all our trumpets speak, give them all breath ...

ACT 5, SCENE 6.

Charles Kean was the first to exploit the pageantry of Shakespeare. He would employ an army of walk-ons, a troupe of dancers, a company of singers, a large orchestra and a host of stage-hands. One of the busiest moments for the crew must have been at the end of the third act of *Macbeth*, where the instructions in Kean's prompt book are: 'Hecate ascends into the air, the witches disappear, then the mist disperses and discovers A Bird's Eye View of the Island of Iona.'

Anthony Hopkins
Hopkins frequently gives the impression that he is a Rotarian pork butcher about to tell the stalls a dirty story.
Felix Barker

When the hurly burly's done ...?

Act 1, Scene 1.

In his diary of a retiring actor, Alec Guinness remembers the actor Henry Baynton giving his Macbeth in 1930. Baynton was known to be a bit of a lush.

On a memorable night of high winds, crashing waves and lashing rain he decided there was time for him to battle his way to the nearest pub while Malcolm and Macduff set about their long tedious scene together, which was followed by Lady M prowling about in her sleep. No Macbeth appeared when Lady M left the stage washing her hands. After a considerable pause the lady stage-manager stepped before the curtain and announced to the bewildered audience – mostly schoolchildren who were studying the play for their exams – 'You can go home now. That is where the play ends.' So they left, rain-coated and capped, doubled up against the elements. Imagine their fright when they saw, blown towards them, the figure of Macbeth in Viking helmet and cross-gartering, black wig flying and beard awry. In a rather hurt, actor-laddie voice he called out to them, 'What? Going home so soon?'

Alec Guinness. *My Name Escapes Me*

Bless you, fair dame!

Act 4, Scene 2.

Ellen Terry wrote to her daughter Edith, regarding the costume she wore as Lady Macbeth at the Lyceum Theatre, 1888.

I wish you could see my dresses. They are superb, especially the first one: green beetles on it, and such a cloak! The dark red hair is fine. The whole thing is Rossetti – rich stained-glass effects. I play some of it well, but, of course, I don't do what I want to do yet. Meanwhile I shall not budge an inch in the reading of it, for that I know is right. Oh, it's such fun, but it's precious hard work, for I by no means make her a 'gentle, loveable woman' as some of 'em say. That's all pickles. I have to what is vulgarly called 'sweat at it,' each night.

Ellen Terry. *The Story of My Life.*

Wherefore could I not pronounce ...?

Act 2, Scene 2.

*In 1972, the Polish film director Roman Polanski directed a film of Macbeth with a
cast of English actors. It was backed by Hugh Hefner of Playboy and filmed on the hillsides
of Wales. Clement Freud interviewed Polanski for an article, wickedly reproducing his
speech patterns phonetically. When the article appeared Polanski fired off a letter to Freud.*

Zis piece about me feelming Macbet vas vonderful, very funny. But being a Pole I
deedn't know zet I speak viz accent of Austrian psychiatrist ... Look, ven Hugh Hefner
reads zis article he vill say, 'How can ziz alien parrot direct our mooovie!' Zo, I am in
beeg trouble ...'

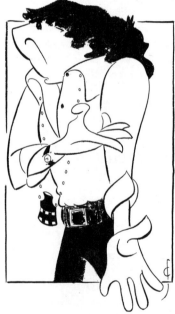

On location, Polanski's accent did occasionally cause trouble.

In the appalling weather, when directorial instructions were barely audible, he had set
up a complicated sequence in which rain, actors, animals, chickens and a farm cart all

had to be cued for the scene. He shouted through the bullhorn.

'OK, cue rain ... people move ... OK ... chickens; get those fucking chickens moving ... right, rain, cue the rain and now ... cut!'

Everything halted. Polanski screamed, 'Why have you stopped ... that was exactly right.' His assistant pointed out that he had called 'Cut!'

'No, I didn't,' yelled Polanski. 'I said "Cut!" I meant "Cut". Cut. Bring on the Cut.'

'You mean cart,' said his assistant.

'Yes ... cut,' said Polanski.

John Parker. *Polanski.*

Making the green one red ...
ACT 2, SCENE 2.

While Nicola McAuliffe was rehearsing Lady M. for Regents Park Open Air Theatre in 1991, she decided that, rather than hover her hands over a candle, it would be more effective to pop them into a bowl of fire, instead.

So Ali Bongo, of the Magician's Circle, was consulted and he suggested an illusion created with a solution of borax. But Miss McAuliffe would have none of that – she wanted the real thing. Apparently a fire-resistant gel had been demonstrated on BBC's *Tomorrow's World*, which, once coated on the flesh, would resist temperatures of up to 600 C. The manufacturers were very helpful but felt they had to point out that the only gel they had left was green, all their flesh-coloured stock having been sent to Pinewood for *Alien 3*.

With the exception of the dialogue, the performance was almost exactly the play of Shakespeare.

Morning Chronicle, 3rd August, 1809.

It provokes the desire but it takes away the performance.

Act 2, Scene 3.

The great William McGonagall's stage debut was as Macbeth at Mr Giles's Theatre in Dundee. Not realising what a talent McGonagall had, Mr Giles said that he could only appear if a large sum of money was paid to the theatre in cash before the performance.

McGonagall said he considered this 'rather hard', but his fellow workers at the Seafield Handloom Works in Dundee had a whip round. They had heard him reciting Shakespeare at work, in his own unique way, and were keen to see him turned loose amidst professional actors.

'When the great night arrived,' McGonagall wrote in his diary, 'my shopmates were in high glee with the hope of getting a Shakespearean treat from me. And I can assure you, without boasting, they were not disappointed.'

When he appeared on stage, he was received with a perfect storm of applause. When he uttered his first line – 'So foul and fair a day I have not seen' – there was a deafening ovation.

The high spot came in the final scene, when Macduff is supposed to kill Macbeth in a sword fight. Unwisely the actor playing Macduff told McGonagall to 'cut it short'.

Suspecting that the actor was jealous of the acclaim he was receiving, McGonagall refused to die. A new ending to Macbeth seemed imminent.

'I continued the combat till he was fairly exhausted, and there was one old gentleman in the audience who cried out: "Well done, McGonagall! Walk into him!" And so I did until he (Macduff) was in a great rage, and stamped his foot, and cried out "Fool! Why don't you fall?" And when I did fall the cry was "McGonagall! McGonagall! Bring him out! Bring him out!" Until I had to come out and receive an ovation from the audience.

Stephen Pile. *Book of Heroic Failures.*

What purgative drug
Would scour these English hence?
Act 5, Scene 3

I don't know if you ever came across a play of Shakespeare's called *Macbeth*? If you did, you may remember this bird Macbeth bumps off another bird named Banquo and gives a big dinner to celebrate, and picture his embarrassment when about the first of the gay throng to turn up is Banquo's ghost, all merry and bright, covered in blood. It gave him a pretty nasty start, I can tell you.

P.G. Wodehouse, *Nothing Serious.*

So foul and fair a day
I have not seen.

ACT 1, SCENE 3.

It's dress-rehearsal night tonight
For '*The Tragedy of Macbeth*';
Dustmen, lawyers and barmaids hang
On one another's breath –
Oh, amateur dramatics is
A leveller. Like death.

Macbeth himself is fifty-nine,
But he always gets the lead
Because he's ... well, he's very good,
He's very good ... indeed.
And he gave a lot of money when
The company was in need.

His make-up is an orange mask,
Beaded with sweat and stiff;
His eyes so deeply etched with black
It looks almost as if
Two exhausted ravens had flung themselves
Into a sandstone cliff.

King Duncan sits with a drooping fag
Beneath the 'No Smoking' signs
Making paper aeroplanes
From last year's set designs.
The prompter's the only one with nerves –
Well, she'll have most of the lines.

Something's happening to the lights –
The illumination's nil,
And all the cast have wandered off
Knowing there's hours to kill
For, whatever's wrong with the dimmer-board
The electrician's dimmer still.

And in the number three dressing-room
The blonde from the Abbey Life
And the local Co-op manager
Who's playing the Thane of Fife
Are doing ... some improvisations based
On being man and wife.

The producer stamps and slams about
With a face like a crumpled bun,
Not because if they started now
They still wouldn't finish till one,
But she just can't seem to command respect
Though she once spoke to Trevor Nunn.

Tempers are frayed, there are tears and sulks
The mascara starts to run;
There are screams from number three dressing- room
Where talk of divorce has begun;
Rows and arguments bubble and boil
But if you ask anyone
Why go through this three times a year?
Why not give up and be done?
They'll all reply, without word of a lie,

'Well, it's such enormous fun!'

Nigel Forde. *No More Fluffy Dice For Me.*

Contending 'gainst obedience ...
Act 2, Scene 4.

Joe, a young child actor, was trained to take the part of the baby King in Kemble's *Macbeth*. Having successfully emerged from rehearsals, he waited nervously in the wings for his scene with the great man.

The possibility that the tragedian would alarm the child on approaching him, stern of aspect and weird of voice, had not been taken into account; and when Kemble, as the gloomy monarch, demanded to know what form was this that rose like the issue of a king, and wore upon its baby brow the round and top of sovereignty – poor Joe was so struck dumb with terror that he just stared, motionless. Kemble glared and muttered madly, 'Speak, boy, speak. Why the devil don't you speak?' The child terrified, shrieked, 'Let me down, I want to go home.' His request had to be complied with; and to Kemble's disgust, the audience was convulsed with laughter.

Henry Francis Whitfeld. *1900.*

Full o'the milk of human-kindness.
Act 1, Scene 5.

One of the great 18th-century stage partnerships, was that of David Garrick and Mrs. Hannah Pritchard. Although not a great beauty, in fact, according to Dr Johnson she was downright plain, Mrs. Pritchard proved to be a revelation when it came to playing Lady Macbeth. The role possessed her so much that she would fall into uncontrollable fits backstage, which she would find hard to shake off, and much to the annoyance of her fellow actors, become wracked with violent sobbing on stage. But she was able to prove her might as an actress, when she shared the stage with Garrick. Together they made a terrifying partnership. And when she retired from the stage in 1758, he never played the part again.

She was once asked for her appraisal of the entire play, to which Mrs Pritchard is reported to have said:

'I do not know as I have never read *Macbeth* further than the sleepwalking scene, and once I have performed that, I always retire and go home to bed.'

Encounter thee with their hearts' thanks ...
Act 3, Scene 4.

PEACH: *(The director of the Farndale Avenue, Townswomen's Guild.)*
I don't know about you, but those witches terrified the life out of me. They did. I'm sure they're all charming ladies in real life, but, goodness me, I'm going to find it difficult to get to sleep tonight, I can tell you. Now, what about the other performances?

Macbeth. Yes, here was a very rousing portrayal. Plenty of light and shade. Lady Macbeth – another well-rounded characterisation.

I wonder, incidentally, how many of you realised that this part was played by a man. Remarkable, isn't it? An excellent Banquo. Bit of trouble with projection. But, good heavens, what a wealth of feeling in those eyes. Something amateurs tend to forget so often. Macduff I liked enormously. A lovely touch, wasn't it, to symbolise her crippled spirit by playing the part on crutches? And I'd like to single this actress out because, she was very, very successful in communicating Macduff's pain. In fact it was quite the most painful performance I've ever seen. My only quibble with the production was that, for me, it lacked a sense of ... comedy. But let's not harp on this. I've had a most enlightening evening, and I think the best thing I can say in summation is that tonight's production makes me feel like going home and re-reading the play.

David McGillivray and Walter Zerlin Jnr.

So weary with disasters ...
Act 3, Scene 1.

Mr Phelps, as Macbeth, came upon the stage [Drury Lane, 1867] with the martial stride and dignity that characterized this excellent actor, and the weird sisters summoned their phantom confederates to appear. When at last one of the apparitions slowly rose to the surface, only to disappear suddenly without giving Macbeth warning, or receiving any himself, there was a slight crash, but nobody was hurt. Next came the passing by of the six ghostly kings, the first of whom lost his crown, and in stooping to recover it was run down by the other five monarchs, who came so rapidly upon the heels of their leader that the several dynasties were all in a heap, creating a spiritual revolution that fairly convulsed the audience. In the last scene, just as Mr. Phelps had given orders to have his banners hung on the outer wall, that frail edifice gave way before it was besieged, and tumbled the King of Scotland into the middle of the stage, where, with uplifted claymore and in a sitting posture, he presented a sight of harmless indignation that would have revenged Macduff for the murder of his entire family!

Joseph Jefferson, *Autobiography, 1890*

To be baited with the rabble's curse ...

ACT 5, SCENE 6

Charles Macklin's appearance was enough to put the fear of God into anybody, and as Macbeth he must have been terrifying. One evening he played the Thane in front of a rowdy and hostile gang of spectators. He was so angered by the disturbance, that he leapt into the audience, his pock-marked face suffused with rage, demanding satisfaction from any that crossed his path. He ran around the gallery like a mad-man, challenging men and women alike. Encountering Mr Skinner, he demanded instant satisfaction. He then rushed into the lobby, tore off his cape, red coat, and striped flannel waistcoat and assumed a fighting stance. Unable to provoke the astonished Mr Skinner, he stormed up to a vast Mrs McDonnell, then in an advanced state of pregnancy, and roundly abused her. Soon afterwards the most conspicuous of the rioters were ejected, and the actors gallantly struggled through the performance, but the tumult throughout the evening was such that the play might have been a pantomime. The events of the night convinced the managers that to allow another performance of *Macbeth* was to court disaster.

Macklin played Macbeth at the age of 75. Unfortunately the public had turned against him for stealing the part from another actor, and hissed him off the stage. The performance had to be interrupted amidst the most unconscionable din. The manager of Covent Garden, George Coleman, came forward and addressed the audience.

'Is it your pleasure that Mr Macklin be discharged?' he asked. Loud cheers and cries of 'yes, yes, yes.'

'Very well,' said Coleman, 'he is discharged.' And thus, in front of the very audience whom he had entertained so loyally and so successfully for a number of years, the great actor was sacked.

Macklin in fact retired from the stage at the age of 89, he had little choice in the matter. He was in the middle of Shylock's famous plea, 'Hath not a Jew eyes ...' when he found to his horror that he had been seized with a 'terrible terror of the mind.' Turning to his audience he assured them 'that this would be the last night of appearing before them in so ridiculous a situation.'

Nothing in his life became him like the leaving it.

ACT 1, SCENE 4

Charles Macklin, 'the wild Irishman,
whose appearance was enough to make a loving mother's heart stand still'.

The great Mexican tragedian Don Edgardo Colonna, alias Edgar Chalmers, once played Macbeth at the Vic during the 1890s. He was so shockingly bad that the audience would not permit him to finish. When he argued that they must let him continue as he was on the point of murdering Duncan, they told him in no uncertain terms to 'Go Home. And leave the poor old King alone!'

The raven himself is hoarse

ACT 1, SCENE 5.

In 1974 Nicol Williamson gave an impressive and much-heralded performance of Macbeth at Stratford.

Unfortunately at one particular schools' matinee the young audience were more interested in talking to each other than in watching the play. The incessant chatter and giggling became so unbearable that after a while Williamson could tolerate it no longer. He threw down the stool he was holding, turned upon the rows of startled school children and told them quite forcibly to 'Shut up!'

'Listen!' he said. 'I could be earning thousands of pounds a week making a film in America if I wanted to, but instead I've chosen to come to Stratford-upon-Avon, for next to nothing, to act in this great and wonderful play – so you could do us all an enormous favour by shutting up whilst I'm doing it. I promise you, if there is so much as another whisper from any of you I will start the play again from the very beginning and will continue to do so until everybody is quiet.'

Come like shadows, so depart.

ACT 4, SCENE 1.

As the stunned audience left the Old Vic, after the opening night of Peter O'Toole's performance, one extremely disgruntled man was heard to say to his wife, 'I expect the dog's been sick in the car as well.'

ACKNOWLEDGEMENTS

Clive Francis would like to thank the following for permission to reproduce copyright material. Every effort has been made to trace and contact all copyright holders but he apologises for any errors or omissions and, if informed, would be glad to make corrections in future editions.

Michael Green and Samuel French Ltd, *The Art of Coarse Acting*. (Copyright Michael Green, 1964)
John Houseman and Simon & Schuster, *Run-Through*. (Copyright John Houseman, 1972)
John Gielgud and Hodder & Stoughton, *Early Stages*. (Copyright The Estate of John Gielgud, 1948)
Paul Eddington and Hodder & Stoughton, *So Far, So Good*. (Copyright The Estate of Paul Eddington,
     1995)
*Simone Signoret and Weidenfeld and Nicolson, Nostalgia Ain't What It Used To Be.
     (Copright Simone Signoret, 1978)*
Nick Page and Harper Collins, *The Tabloid Shakespeare*. (Copyright Nick Page, 1999)
James Agate and Harrap, *The Selective Ego*. (Copyright The Estate of James Agate)
Donald Sinden and Hodder & Stoughton, *A Touch of the Memoirs*. (Copyright Donald Sinden)
Alec Guinness and Hamish Hamilton, *My Name Escapes Me*. (Copyright Alec Guinness, 1996)
Michael Meyer and Martin Secker & Warburg, *Not Prince Hamlet*. (Copyright, Michael Meyer, 1989)
John Parker and Gollancz, *Polanski*. (Copyright John Parker, 1993)
Also to Malcom MacKee for writing the song 'There is Nothing Like a Thane' especially for this publication.

Every effort has been made to locate the owners of copyright for extracts included in this book, but not always with success. Acknowledgement is therefore necessary to the following, or their heirs, from whom we would be glad to hear:
Donald Wolfit: *First Interval* (Odhams, 1955); Paul Griffin: *How To Be Ridiculously Well-Read In One Evening*, edited by E.O. Parrott (Viking,1989); Stephen Pile: *Book of Heroic Failures* (Routledge and Kegan Paul, 1979)

INDEX

Fan our people cold
ACT 1, SCENE 2.

The curtain drew up for Macbeth:
I paused between glory and sorrow –
Says I: 'I'm resolved upon death,
But I'll just put it off till to-morrow.'

Thomas Love Peacock *c 1818*